S0-BBC-238

# In His Service

## A Guide to Christian Living in the Military

## By Rick Bereit

**dawson**media

P.O. Box 6000, Colorado Springs, CO 80934

A MINISTRY OF THE NAVIGATORS

*In His Service: A Guide to Christian Living in the Military*
By Rick Bereit

© 2002 Rick Bereit. All rights reserved. No part of this publication may be reproduced in any form without written permission from Dawson Media, P.O. Box 6000, Colorado Springs, CO 80934.

Published by

**dawson**media

a ministry of The Navigators, P.O. Box 6000, Colorado Springs, CO 80934

The Navigators is an international Christian organization. Jesus Christ gave His followers the Great Commission to go and make disciples (Matthew 28:19). The aim of The Navigators is to help fulfill that commission by multiplying laborers for Christ in every nation.

Dawson Media is a ministry of The Navigators that aims to help Navigator staff and laypeople create and experiment with new ministry tools for personal evangelism and discipleship.

Editor: Leura Jones
Proofreader: Tricia Bennett
Cover design: Steve Learned
Cover photo: Courtesy of the U.S. Department of Defense. U.S. Navy photo by Chief Warrant Officer 2 Seth Rossman.

Printed in the United States of America
ISBN: 0-9672480-5-1

Unless otherwise noted, all Scriptures are taken from the *Holy Bible: New International Version*® (NIV®). Copyright © 1973, 1978, 1984 by International Bible Society. Other versions, using the following abbreviations, include: *King James Version* (KJV); *The New Testament in Modern English*, J.B. Phillips Translator (PHILLIPS), © J.B. Phillips 1958, 1960, 1972, used by permission of MacMillan Publishing Company; and *The New Testament: An Expanded Translation by Kenneth S. Wuest* (WUEST) © 1961 Wm. B. Eerdmans Publishing Co.

w.dawsonmedia.com

*In memory of my father, Arnold E. Bereit,
military aviator, loving husband, family leader,
and the man who taught me most about life
by the power of his example.*

# Contents

FOREWORD ................................................................................vii

ACKNOWLEDGMENTS ...........................................................ix

INTRODUCTION ......................................................................xiii

PART I: THE MILITARY WAY OF LIFE
1   Why a Military? .................................................................3
2   Combat .............................................................................15
3   Basic Training ..................................................................23
4   A Warrior's Work ............................................................31
5   Promotion, Pay, and Contentment .................................41
6   Assignments and Moves .................................................49
7   Professional Development ...............................................61

PART II: THE FRUITFUL CHRISTIAN LIFE
8   A Vital Relationship with God .......................................71
9   Evangelism .......................................................................83
10  Making Disciples .............................................................93
11  Chaplains, Chapels, Churches, and Organizations ........105
12  Servanthood in the Service .............................................117
13  Pursuing Excellence ........................................................127
14  Family Matters .................................................................139

PART III: THE VICTORIOUS CHRISTIAN LIFE
15  Fellowship ........................................................................149
16  The Enemy Within ..........................................................157
17  Moral Minefields .............................................................167
18  Individuality and Conformity .........................................177
19  Time Management ...........................................................183
20  Principles of War .............................................................193
21  Onward Christian Soldiers .............................................209

# Foreword

RECENTLY, I WAS SPEAKING at a Europe-wide Protestant Men of the Chapel (EPMOC) conference in Germany. When asked why I had accepted speaking at the conference, in light of my intense schedule and the demands in my role as president of The Navigators, I replied, "Because I have been called to minister in and to the military."

For 37 years (13½ active; 23½ reserve) I served, not for financial gain or position, but because I believe God led me to do so. Mary's and my military life was transformed by the influence of godly men and women who helped us learn how to live in this special place and also by the many godly chaplains who served us and opened the door for us to serve.

Rick Bereit feels deeply this same call to the military. For 30 years, Rick and his wife, Barb, have lived the reality of what he writes about so well in this book. You can almost smell the "smoke of battle" as Rick writes not from theory or idealism, but from the trenches.

Every place of work is a mission field, but the military is unique: Friendships span decades, your reputation precedes you in an assignment, and you experience incredible openness and opportunity. Yet just "being there" is not sufficient. As with any endeavor, effectively following Christ in the military requires effort. And effort must be married to knowledge and coaching. Rick provides these brilliantly in *In His Service*. These principles apply to all ranks, all services, and all ages. They can be adapted to wherever God puts you. I only wish this book had been available to me when I first entered the military.

I have known Rick since he was a student at the U.S. Air Force Academy and involved in our Navigator ministry there. I have never known a time when he was not wholehearted in his commitment to God. Throughout his military career, Rick constantly put Christ first and lived out the principles he shares in this book. I have the utmost respect for him as a friend, fellow Air Force officer, and brother in Christ. I pray his words will challenge you, encourage you, and help you make the military your personal mission field.


Jerry White
Major General, USAF (ret)
President, The Navigators

# Acknowledgments

FEW ACCOMPLISHMENTS OF SIGNIFICANCE are achieved alone. This book is no exception. From the seed thoughts to the finished volume, I have had the help of godly, wise, and gifted people.

While I was a student at the U.S. Air Force Academy, two instructors, in particular, modeled Christian character and well-balanced service to God and country. Major (eventually Major General) Jerry White and Captain Roger Brandt were my mentors, teaching me by their example the important principles of being a disciple of Jesus and a quality military member. Not only was their "on-duty" modeling helpful, but time spent with their families also demonstrated to me how wonderful life could be in a Christian home. In my last year at the Academy, Jerry White assembled the soon-to-be lieutenants who had been in his Bible study in the living room of his house. He began to explain the realities of military life and tips on living a consistent life in that environment. Those discussions formed the seed thoughts that eventually grew into this book.

While I was writing the book, I sent completed chapters to a small group of close friends and committed Christians. Each one of them, from their own unique perspective, gave me feedback on readability and content. Their ideas and guidance are imbedded deeply in these pages. They are a talented and diverse group:

Neal Crossland—CMSgt (retired). First Sergeant, outstanding enlisted leader, and long-time personal friend.

Jonna King—Captain (junior officer). Godly female officer and talented leader and manager. Mother of two (at the time of writing) and married to another military member. A lady with exceptional capacities.

Jim Hough—Lt. Col., chaplain, former Navy enlisted man. Deep longing for close fellowship with God and tremendous sensitivity to the needs of enlisted men and women. Tremendous insight on being a chaplain in the military.

Dan Schoenborn—Long-time Navigator missionary to military men and women. Former Air Force enlisted technician. Great understanding of the pressures of family, duty to country, and service in the Kingdom.

Brent Smeltzer—Lt. Col. (retired), former enlisted contracting specialist. Has an intense hunger for God's Word and its practical, daily application. Analytical mind and deep-caring person.

In addition to these who read every word of every chapter, several others reviewed one or more chapters and provided invaluable feedback. These included my son, Captain Derek Bereit; Colonel (retired) Ron Andrea, long-time friend and fellow commander; and my pastor in Montgomery, Alabama, Dr. Joe Godfrey.

I would like to particularly commend my oldest daughter, Kristine (Bereit) Stark. As I began to write this book, she was living in our home while her husband attended basic training and technical military training. Each afternoon, Kristine would return home from her teaching job and greet me with the question, "How much did you get done on the book today, Dad?" I would give her a chapter or a fragment, whatever I had completed that day. She would read not only for content, but would also proof it for grammar and syntax. She was the spark plug that kept the machinery running during the hardest part of putting initial thoughts and ideas on paper.

# ACKNOWLEDGMENTS

Especially, I thank my wife, Barbara, for her encouragement—not only to keep plugging while writing the book, but also for her total and unwavering support of me, and each of our four children, as we lived 30 "wandering" years in the military. We moved 17 times in those 30 years! Many of the family comments in the book flow directly from her behavior and attitude. She has been a supportive partner in every activity I ever attempted.

Mike Schmid, a member of The Navigators' Military Leadership Team, played a key role in moving this book from idea to reality. He was the first to read the complete draft. He saw merit in the effort and worked tirelessly to find the best venues for publishing and distributing the book.

I owe more than I could express to Leura Jones, my editor at Dawson Media. She has graciously and tactfully made a difficult manuscript into a readable book, something future readers will appreciate. She has analyzed content, organization, flow, and impact with her exceptional editing gifts. Thanks also to Steve Learned, at Dawson Media, for layout, art, and other assistance that shaped my efforts into a book.

Finally, I want to acknowledge the essential role of the Spirit of God in guiding me to write this book. From time to time, His prompting during my military career would cause me to look back on and analyze an event, which often ended up in my journal. He often brought Scriptures to mind that clearly taught the essential points in each chapter. Even as I was putting ink on paper, I sensed His presence and guidance. I felt more like a scribe, recording other's words and thoughts, than an author.

To each of these and to several I have not named specifically who participated in research, review, and encouragement, I am truly grateful. Your work has resulted in a book that is much needed by Christian warriors as they serve God and country.

# Introduction

GOD HAS CALLED MEN AND WOMEN in every walk of life to live obedient lives among our peers. When we do this, we reflect the life of Jesus, a shining light in a dark world. Jesus said, "Go and make disciples of all nations" (Matthew 28:19). His command requires going into every nation, but it also implies reaching into every walk of life. That includes the military.

In many ways, military people serve in a foreign culture. The military has its own rules, values, and language. It demands more order, structure, and conformity than civilian life. The military, unlike other jobs, is not something you show up to periodically. It's not like working *for* IBM or Nabisco. You don't work *for* the military; you're *in it!* It is a way of life that envelopes you. It makes extensive demands on your abilities, time, and, unlike most professions, your life! The first line of the Code of Conduct for U.S. Military Forces reads:

> I am an American, fighting in the forces, which guard my country and our way of life. I am prepared to *give my life* in their defense.

When you join the military, you swear to surrender your life, if necessary, in defense of your country. Life-and-death responsibilities accompany the privilege of serving in the military, making it a profession like no other.

The military is an organization that never sleeps, never

takes a holiday. It is a society of nomads who are exposed to many cultures and countries but who never stay in one place long enough to put down roots. Yet it also brings people together in a way most civilians never experience. Close living quarters, shared adversity, and group achievements lead to life-long relationships. Friendships run deep and cross traditional barriers of race, color, class, and background.

The best way to reach this culture is from the inside. God leads some Christians to be part of the military and to share the Gospel within this context. No matter what you may have heard about the vices and challenges of military life, it *is* possible to live a consistent, obedient, godly life while serving faithfully as a warrior. This book, designed as a resource to turn to throughout your military years, will show you how.

Part I describes military life and how it is culturally different from life outside the military. Intended primarily for new and prospective warriors, it reconciles obedience to Christ with military service and will help you understand the requirements and benefits of military life. Parts II and III provide practical insights for living a fruitful and victorious life in the military.

Thousands of men and women have served in the military as active, fulfilled Christians. Some make a career of the military, serving God and advancing His Kingdom through decades of military service. Whether your service is short or long, whether you are an officer or enlisted, God can use your time in the military to build your character, stamina, and vision. You will find unlimited ministry opportunities that beckon you to use your God-given talent and spiritual gifts to advance the Gospel and make disciples.

Regardless of your branch of service, your specific tasks, or your length of time in service, my hope is that you will realize, most importantly, that you are *in His service.*

# Part I:
# The Military Way of Life

THE DAY YOU JOIN THE MILITARY, your way of life begins to change dramatically. Conformity, order, and structure become increasingly important. Personal choice and free time decrease. And so the process begins—the military shaping your thoughts, actions, and habits to make you an effective and efficient part of its organization. This transition brings extreme stress and stretching, which challenge even the most prepared.

No doubt about it, the military has its own unique culture—one that is entirely different from that experienced by most Americans. Christians who desire to be relevant and make a spiritual impact in this "foreign" culture must first become immersed in it and understand it. As a member of the military, your immersion into this new culture begins with basic training and continues through your first assignment. The next seven chapters will help you understand the process and the objective that you're aiming toward.

# Why a Military?

*The LORD saw how great man's wickedness on the earth had become, and that every inclination of the thoughts of his heart was only evil all the time (Genesis 6:5).*

*What causes fights and quarrels among you? Don't they come from your desires that battle within you? (James 4:1).*

IMAGINE A WORLD WITH NO WAR. Imagine a place with no soldiers, no guns, no battles. Imagine that there is no history of war and, therefore, no grudges, no retribution, and no "historic enemies." Imagine a world where strong nations always work to protect the weak. Imagine a planet where natural resources are evenly distributed, where nations with *more* willingly share with those that have *less*. While you are imagining, consider what it would be like to live in a world with no locks and no barbed-wire fences. Imagine people who always tell the truth and who work at understanding others. This would be a great world to live in, but it is clearly not our reality.

## A WAR-FILLED WORLD

From the beginning of time, the story of man is a tale of conflict and struggle. Man's endless strife has a single cause at its root: rebellion against God. The root feeds many branches, including idolatry (worshipping man-made creations), personal conflicts (between husband and wife, neighbors, coworkers), and regional and national conflict. Like Adam and Eve, all men and women throughout history have set aside the commands of God, attempting instead to establish their own independent kingdom of "me." The heart houses a host of powerful, self-seeking motivations, which fuel consuming fires of hatred and hostility. Rebellion against God has led to racial prejudice, inordinate national fervor, greed, fear, and jealousy and has resulted in the deaths of millions of people over thousands of years.

Obviously, we don't live in a perfect world. Not only do others not treat us well, we also fall short of our own standards for kindness, mercy, and justice. This is how Jesus described our hearts:

> *"For from within, out of men's hearts, come evil thoughts, sexual immorality, theft, murder, adultery, greed, malice, deceit, lewdness, envy, slander, arrogance and folly"* *(Mark 7:21–22).*

If people have warfare in their own hearts, it's not surprising that the conflict spreads to groups—families, cities, states, nations.

Warfare is not God's first and best plan for humanity. His plan was a perfect garden with no separation. Man and woman enjoyed perfect fellowship with their Creator. When they rebelled against God, the perfection of His first plan was broken. The consequences of their choice brought pain in childbirth, hard labor to get food from the earth, and death. Signaling the beginning of God's much less attractive plan for human beings, He closed the gate to the garden and posted an armed guard (Genesis 3:24).

From the earliest times, families and tribes have developed weapons to attack others and defend themselves. Over the centuries, conflicts expanded from family feuds to national wars, and the means of warfare became conglomerated, organized, and refined. Militaries became separate "organizations" with distinct people, leadership, and mission.

## FIGHTING FOR A MORAL CAUSE

Today, militaries are organized national forces that secure and defend national objectives. Military force can be used for moral, altruistic purposes or for self-seeking, immoral purposes. Every Christian who contemplates military service must answer the question, "Is my nation and military seeking noble objectives?" If not, then the Christian must refuse to serve, at all costs, in a military whose aims are immoral or illegal. Throughout the centuries, Christians who have contemplated military service have had to consider the morality and correctness of national objectives.

If you are a soldier nearing a battlefield, a sailor steaming toward a battle at sea, or an airman closing in on an aerial dogfight, you want to know that "right" is on your side. You want to hold the moral high ground. If possible, you'd like to know God is on your side and plans to give you victory. General Joshua, leading the armies of Israel, had this encounter with the commander of the Lord's army:

> Now when Joshua was near Jericho, he looked up and saw a man standing in front of him with a drawn sword in his hand. Joshua went up to him and asked, "Are you for us or for our enemies?" "Neither," he replied, "but as commander of the army of the LORD I have now come." Then Joshua fell facedown to the ground in reverence, and asked him, "What message does my Lord have for his servant?" (Joshua 5:13–14, emphasis added).

Joshua wanted to know whose side God's warrior was on. The angelic commander's answer is important. He claimed to be on God's side, not the side of either combatant. God does not join *us* in *our purposes*. We either join or refuse to join *Him* in *His purposes*. This is an encounter worth remembering. God does not belong to a nation, nor does His protection and favor belong to one nation. This was illustrated clearly in the commands He gave to the emerging nation of Israel. God made this general promise to the army:

> *When you go to war against your enemies and see horses and chariots and an army greater than yours, do not be afraid of them, because the LORD your God, who brought you up out of Egypt, will be with you. When you are about to go into battle, the priest shall come forward and address the army. He shall say: "Hear, O Israel, today you are going into battle against your enemies. Do not be fainthearted or afraid; do not be terrified or give way to panic before them. For the LORD your God is the one who goes with you to fight for you against your enemies to give you victory" (Deuteronomy 20:1–4).*

God promised to give them victory. At the end of the book of Deuteronomy, however, we see that this was a conditional promise based on Israel's obedience to God's righteous purposes.

### *Blessings with obedience*

> *If you fully obey the LORD your God and carefully follow all his commands I give you today, the LORD your God will set you high above all the nations on earth. All these blessings will come upon you and accompany you if you obey the LORD your God. . . . The LORD will grant that the enemies who rise up against you will be defeated before you. They will come at you from one direction but flee from you in seven (Deuteronomy 28:1–2, 7).*

### *Curses with disobedience*

> *However, if you do not obey the LORD your God and do not
> carefully follow all his commands and decrees I am giv-
> ing you today, all these curses will come upon you and
> overtake you: You will be cursed in the city and cursed in
> the country. . . . The LORD will cause you to be defeated
> before your enemies. You will come at them from one
> direction but flee from them in seven, and you will
> become a thing of horror to all the kingdoms on earth.
> Your carcasses will be food for all the birds of the air and
> the beasts of the earth, and there will be no one to
> frighten them away (Deuteronomy 28:15–16, 25–26).*

## WAR AND OBEDIENCE TO GOD

In America, our military oath of allegiance is to support and
defend the Constitution of the United States. Our military fights
to preserve democracy and freedom. This helps you, the combatant, focus on the big picture. Throughout the history of our
nation, many Christians have reconciled national objectives
with personal obedience to God. Even during the American Civil
War, Christians on both sides reconciled their military service
with their relationship to God. Those who could not, however,
dissented and refused to fight. During each war, some citizens
have refused to participate in combat for moral and ethical reasons. You must decide to serve or not serve based on your
understanding of the moral and ethical objectives.

Do the national objectives mesh with righteousness and
truth? This is the most important thing you will consider. You
must be convinced that military service is consistent with your
own internal values. You must believe national objectives are
just and moral. Modern military recruiting has emphasized positive aspects of peacetime service—educational benefits, leadership experience, adventure, technical training, and exciting

travel. While these may be factors, the first hurdle every potential soldier must clear is this: "Does military service conflict
with my deepest personal values?" Only after deciding this can
you begin to evaluate the other benefits.

## WHAT DOES THE BIBLE SAY?

What about the sixth commandment, "Thou shalt not kill"?
Clearly, this is not a universal command against all killing
because a few verses later, God prescribed death by stoning for
several offenses against society. Bible scholars concur the best
translation of the words "not kill" is "not murder." The *New
International Version* records the verse this way:

> *You shall not murder (Exodus 20:13).*

What God prohibits in the sixth commandment is the
unlawful taking of life by an individual. In limited civil cases and
for soldiers, God permitted the taking of life. But even these
exceptions have limits. It is possible for soldiers to commit murder. The Bible, as well as international law, for instance, condemn the slaughter of prisoners.

What does the Bible say specifically about war? It is clear
from many verses that warfare is an enduring feature of life on
earth. It has existed, it will continue for a time, and then there
will be an end to warfare. A few passages illustrate this.

### War exists

> *There is a time for everything, and a season for every
> activity under heaven: a time to kill and a time to heal, a
> time to tear down and a time to build, a time to love and
> a time to hate, a time for war and a time for peace (Eccle-
> siastes 3:1, 3, 8).*

*From early times the prophets who preceded you and me have prophesied war, disaster and plague against many countries and great kingdoms (Jeremiah 28:8).*

*I saw heaven standing open and there before me was a white horse, whose rider is called Faithful and True. With justice he judges and makes war (Revelation 19:11).*

### War will continue

*"You will hear of wars and rumors of wars, but see to it that you are not alarmed. Such things must happen, but the end is still to come. Nation will rise against nation, and kingdom against kingdom. There will be famines and earthquakes in various places. All these are the beginning of birth pains" (Matthew 24:6–8).*

*War will continue until the end, and desolations have been decreed (Daniel 9:26b).*

### War will cease

*He will judge between many peoples and will settle disputes for strong nations far and wide. They will beat their swords into plowshares and their spears into pruning hooks. Nation will not take up sword against nation,* nor will they train for war anymore *(Micah 4:3, emphasis added).*

*And I heard a loud voice from the throne saying, "Now the dwelling of God is with men, and he will live with them. They will be his people, and God himself will be with them and be their God. He will wipe every tear from their eyes.* There will be no more death or mourning or crying or pain, *for the old order of things has passed away." He who was seated on the throne said, "I am making everything new!" Then he said, "Write this down, for these words are trustworthy and true" (Revelation 21:3–5, emphasis added).*

## SHOULD CHRISTIANS BE INVOLVED?

It's clear that war exists and that it will not cease until God brings it to a close. But should Christians be involved? Maybe you wonder if this plan of God calls for the wicked to fight against each other and for Christians to stay out of it.

These are good questions. Christians throughout history have decided on both sides of the issue. Some have concluded that Christianity and military service are incompatible; others felt that Christian principles allowed military service. Let's look at some of the Scriptures that address this issue.

On occasions, God appeared to men and instructed them to fight a battle. God trained, directed, and assisted them, thereby ensuring victory. The Bible has many examples in which God used warfare to accomplish His purposes. Look at the lives of Joshua, Gideon, Saul, and David. These men were from Israel and today are considered "God's warriors." But God also commanded men from other nations, including Nebuchadnezzar and Cyrus.

Moreover, war is not solely an earthly event. God has seen war in heaven! There will be another battle in heaven before all war is finished.

*And there was war in heaven. Michael and his angels fought against the dragon, and the dragon and his angels fought back (Revelation 12:7).*

War in heaven has spilled over to earth. Many of our wars are rooted in a struggle between good and evil. For example, we can certainly see a difference in objectives between Allied forces and Axis powers during World War II. One alliance sought world dominance, practiced racial discrimination, and murdered millions of its own "unwanted" people. This is not to say Allied soldiers did no evil, nor does it suppose every soldier in the Axis armies was wicked and cruel. The overall characterization of the two forces, however, was one of good and evil. God used one group of nations to defeat the evil caused by others.

The war in heaven will spill over and combine with war on the earth once again. The two wars are not really separate; they are the same war being conducted on separate battlefields. But in the end, the heavenly war will be fought on an earthly battlefield.

*I saw* heaven *standing open and there before me was a white horse, whose rider is called Faithful and True. With justice he judges and makes war. His eyes are like blazing fire, and on his head are many crowns. He has a name written on him that no one knows but he himself. He is dressed in a robe dipped in blood, and his name is the Word of God. The armies of heaven were following him, riding on white horses and dressed in fine linen, white and clean. Out of his mouth comes a sharp sword with which to strike down* the nations. *"He will rule them with an iron scepter." He treads the winepress of the fury of the wrath of God Almighty (Revelation 19:11–15, emphasis added).*

### WHAT DID JESUS DO?

Jesus, during His life and ministry, had opportunities to declare the military profession "off-limits." To the woman caught in adultery, He said, "Go and sin no more." He could have given these same instructions to the Roman centurion in Matthew 8, but He didn't. If Jesus wanted to condemn the profession of arms for all time, this encounter provided the ideal opportunity. Instead, He commended the Roman soldier for his faith, though he was a soldier from an invading army.

*When Jesus had entered Capernaum, a centurion came to him, asking for help. "Lord," he said, "my servant lies at home paralyzed and in terrible suffering." Jesus said to him, "I will go and heal him." The centurion replied, "Lord, I do not deserve to have you come under my roof. But just say the word, and my servant will be healed. For I myself am a man under authority, with soldiers under me. I tell this one, 'Go,' and he goes; and that one, 'Come,' and he comes. I say to my servant, 'Do this,' and he does it." When Jesus heard this, he was astonished and said to those following him, "I tell you the truth,* I have not found anyone in Israel with such great faith" *(Matthew 8:5–10, emphasis added).*

John the Baptist also had direct communication with soldiers, who asked him how they should show works of righteousness in their lives. This is a vital passage of Scripture for those in the military.

*During the high priesthood of Annas and Caiaphas, the word of God came to John son of Zechariah in the desert. He went into all the country around the Jordan, preaching a baptism of repentance for the forgiveness of sins.... John said to the crowds coming out to be baptized by him, "You brood of vipers! Who warned you to flee from the coming wrath?* Produce fruit in keeping with repentance. *And do not begin to say to yourselves, 'We have Abraham as our father.' For I tell you that out of these stones God can raise up children for Abraham."* ... *Then some* soldiers asked him, *"And what should we do?" He replied, "Don't extort money and don't accuse people falsely—be content with your pay" (Luke 3:2–3, 7–8, 14, emphasis added).*

This was an important question from the military sector of

society. What should soldiers do to "produce fruit in keeping with repentance"? John could have said many things, including, "Get out of the military. It's immoral, and you shouldn't be involved!" But he didn't. Speaking as a prophet, under the inspiration of God, he told soldiers not to abuse their power and to lead honest, content lives. This is profound.

Both Jesus and John the Baptist could have condemned military service as an option for men and women of God, but they did not.

### MAKING YOUR CHOICE

To serve honestly and consistently in the military, you must be convinced of the "rightness" of your nation's objectives and their alignment with your own beliefs. Be clear in your own mind what you believe about the morality of warfare and Christians serving in the military. Take time to read and consider these and other biblical principles. Be sure *what* you believe and *why*. And as you make your decision, you can be confident of God's approval for those who choose military service.

 **SUMMARY**

- ✦ War is a result of man's rebellion against God.
- ✦ War has existed first in heaven and now on earth, and it will continue until God brings it to a close.
- ✦ Militaries exist to secure national objectives.
- ✦ National objectives can be good or evil, and you should evaluate your nation's military objectives in light of your own beliefs and conscience.
- ✦ The Bible gives examples of how God has used warfare to accomplish His purposes.
- ✦ Although they could have, neither Jesus nor John the Baptist forbid military service to Christians.

# Combat

*A thousand may fall at your side, ten thousand at your right hand, but it will not come near you (Psalm 91:7).*

*But someone drew his bow at random and hit the king of Israel between the sections of his armor. The king told the chariot driver, "Wheel around and get me out of the fighting. I've been wounded" (2 Chronicles 18:33).*

*Precious in the sight of the LORD is the death of his saints (Psalm 116:15).*

THESE VERSES DESCRIBE THREE possible outcomes soldiers face in combat. In the midst of the most intense combat, some soldiers survive without a scratch. Others are wounded. Some are killed. Every soldier, sailor, and airman must comprehend the real possibility of injury or death.

The purpose of military service is to maintain peace by being prepared for war. If that fails, the military is called on to fight. General George Patton observed, "The more an Army sweats in peace, the less it bleeds in war." In recent years, the commander of the Air Force Air Combat Command, General Jumper, reminded his warriors, "Dead targets are our product in war. Our product in peace is sorties that train people to make dead targets." Both quotes point to this reality: Death goes hand in hand with warfare.

## WAR AT A DISTANCE

Recent developments in military technology have, to some extent, depersonalized warfare. A lone aviator flying at high altitude can destroy multiple "targets"—combatants and sometimes noncombatants—in seconds. The aviator will see little of the mayhem and destruction caused by the weapons. This long-distance warfare exists in each of the branches of service. Artillery and naval guns reach beyond the sight of the soldier or sailor. Rockets and missiles deliver incredible destruction with pinpoint accuracy miles from the launcher. Fewer modern-day battles are fought looking the enemy in the eye. At the same time, fewer soldiers are assigned to duties involving combat. Increasing numbers of soldiers perform combat-support functions, such as maintenance, transportation, ordnance, medical, and engineering.

Today, it is possible to forget that the principal purpose of the military is combat, and combat injures and kills people. Recruiting advertisements emphasize educational benefits, the joy of teamwork, leadership challenges, and adventure. In fact, for many in the military, the concept of warrior behavior can become purely philosophical—until warfare begins.

## EXPECT COMBAT

You must remember that as a member of the military, you are, individually and corporately, an instrument of armed warfare. The purpose of all military training and exercises is to produce combat-ready forces that fight to win. The difference between winning and losing a battle is often the small advantage of intensity, ferocity, tenacity, courage, and individual combat skill one opponent has over the other.

You should enter the military expecting to experience combat. You must consider the probability of taking another life or losing your own life at the hands of an enemy. Combat has traditionally been limited to battlefields among uniformed warriors. The distinctions today are not always so clear. In modern times, soldiers have been wounded or killed not only on the battlefield, but also in barracks, aboard ships at anchor, and even while traveling out of uniform on a commercial airplane. Forces at rest in garrison or in port are subject to attack. The ability of the enemy to rapidly and unexpectedly reach out and devastatingly touch opponents has increased. The threat of injury or death is always present; the terror of combat is not reduced with modern weaponry or tactics. If anything, combat has become more frightening with the speed and lethality modern warfare has made possible.

You must ponder your obligation to fight for your nation and your willingness to surrender your own life. This is not a commitment to make lightly. The oath of office includes these words: "I take this obligation freely, without any mental reservation or purpose of evasion." Military service requires unwavering, unflinching dedication to fulfill the obligations of combat.

Jesus said, "Greater love has no one than this, that he lay down his life for his friends" (John 15:13). Jesus demonstrated this by laying down His own life so that His followers might have forgiveness of sin and eternal life. The "Battle Hymn of the Republic" incorporated this theme in the memorable words: "As He died to make men holy, let us live to make men free."

Make no mistake, Jesus' death on the cross was a singularly significant event in the timeless battle between God's quest to love us and Satan's efforts to deny us that love. Jesus the warrior became Christ the Savior in that pivotal battle of this long war. He died to give us life everlasting.

As a soldier, you must realize that if you die, it is a sacrifice that enables others to live. Few soldiers *want* to die. Most want to live, marry, have children, and grow old. However, they realize if no one fights the battles, few will enjoy liberty and peace for long. It would be easier if, when an aggressor mounts an attack, soldiers could line up on the battlefield and persuade the other army to go away. This would preserve life and be much less costly. Unfortunately, there is no historic precedent for the success of this method. More realistically, soldiers hope that diplomatic efforts will resolve differences.

Warriors love peace! And why not? It is *their* blood that is sacrificed to secure victory and peace if diplomacy fails. But, though they love peace, soldiers must constantly be prepared for war. Even if you're a support specialist behind the front lines, you are a legitimate target for the enemy's long-range weapons. When you are taught—as all soldiers are—to fire a weapon, the inference is that you must be prepared to defend yourself. Carrying a weapon makes you a potential target.

## EVERY SOLDIER IS A TARGET

Every service member contributes to the fighting capability of the military. Consequently, each one is a legitimate target for the enemy.

Airman Peters was a brilliant radar repair technician. After one U.S. assignment, he was sent to an overseas location. Shortly after his arrival there, a terrorist organization attempted to penetrate the perimeter fence and destroy aircraft parked at his base. The attackers were captured after a short skirmish, and only a few aircraft were damaged. No one was killed. The Monday following the incident, Airman Peters asked his commander for a discharge. "Why would you want to leave the military?" the commander asked. "You are one of our most promising radar technicians!" The commander was shocked at the answer Peters gave. "I joined the military to learn a skill and get an education," he said. "I never thought *I* would be attacked."

Although this airman's views and level of commitment are not the norm, they're also not uncommon. Some view the military, erroneously, as just another job, missing the important fact that its principal product is formidable defense and violent offense. Anyone who puts on the uniform of military service must realize the nature of war and the possible personal consequences.

## A CHRISTIAN'S COMFORT

As a Christian warrior, you can face the potential of your own death with resolve and comfort. This is possible because of the promises Jesus made about death and eternal life. It is comforting to know that death is precious to the Lord. His promises should not make you flippant or careless but should help you remain effective under life-and-death pressure. Consider the assurance of these promises:

> "I tell you the truth, whoever hears my word and believes him who sent me has eternal life and will not be condemned; he has crossed over from death to life" (John 5:24).

> And this is the testimony: God has given us eternal life, and this life is in his Son. He who has the Son has life; he who does not have the Son of God does not have life. I write these things to you who believe in the name of the Son of God so that you may know that you have eternal life (1 John 5:11–13).

> Jesus said to her, "I am the resurrection and the life. He who believes in me will live, even though he dies" (John 11:25).

As a Christian, you have the assurance of eternal life. This greatly reduces the "sting" of death. Fighting a war thousands of miles from home, risking precious life in combat, is made less traumatic by the assurance of Jesus' presence and His control over your eternal destiny.

**TAKING THE LIFE OF ANOTHER**

As a military warrior, you not only risk your own life but you become a key player in taking the lives of others. You become an instrument of death. Those who serve in combat branches rarely lose sight of this. Those in support branches, however, can sometimes forget that the product of the military is violent combat.

> *"You are my war club, my weapon for battle—with you I shatter nations, with you I destroy kingdoms, with you I shatter horse and rider, with you I shatter chariot and driver" (Jeremiah 51:20–21).*

Understand the requirements of the oath of office. You may be required to take the life of another. This is an immense responsibility. Few movies capture the stark reality of face-to-face combat better than the opening minutes of *Saving Private Ryan*. The earth shakes with artillery explosions. Bodies are torn apart by automatic weapons and shrapnel. The once-beautiful beach is strewn with broken pieces of equipment and bodies. The horrible carnage of military combat has no parallels in life. Even those who have heard others' experiences will not be prepared for the stark reality of taking another life. Sometimes it is face to face and sometimes at a distance. Sometimes it is kill-or-be-killed combat; other times a surprise attack eliminates an enemy before they can respond. Regardless of the conditions, the result is death and destruction. The violence and devastation are immense assaults on the senses. Frequently, warriors "shut down" mentally and emotionally as a means to protect themselves from the pain and suffering.

In a kill-or-be-killed environment, you must have a clear view of what needs to be done and a 100-percent commitment to do it quickly.

*He trains my hands for battle; my arms can bend a bow of bronze. You give me your shield of victory, and your right hand sustains me; you stoop down to make me great. You broaden the path beneath me, so that my ankles do not turn. I pursued my enemies and overtook them; I did not turn back till they were destroyed. I crushed them so that they could not rise; they fell beneath my feet. You armed me with strength for battle; you made my adversaries bow at my feet. You made my enemies turn their backs in flight, and I destroyed my foes (Psalm 18:34–40).*

### THE REALITY OF COMBAT

You may be attracted to many different facets of military life, but keep one fact in mind: The military exists for one purpose: to maintain peace by being prepared for war. Every member of the military contributes directly or indirectly to that end. Expect to be involved in combat during your time in the military. Make every effort to prepare yourself mentally for combat. And when the time comes for combat, trust in God's promise to be with you wherever you go and whatever you face.

### SUMMARY

⊕ The principal purpose of the military is combat.

⊕ Combat is violent and aims to kill or wound the enemy.

⊕ All warriors must consider the possibility they will be required to kill.

⊕ They also must understand that violent injury and death are probabilities of military service.

⊕ God promises to be with us wherever we are and assures His followers of eternal life.

⊕ He can help you overcome fears that would otherwise paralyze you, allowing you to confidently perform your duty as a warrior.

# Basic Training

*He did this only to teach warfare to the descendants of the Israelites who had not had previous battle experience (Judges 3:2).*

BASIC TRAINING TRANSFORMS regular men and women into soldiers. To create effective soldiers, the military methodically instills the warrior spirit and teaches individuals to become team members. "Basic" or "boot camp" is the place where individuals are shaped into cohesive military teams.

Basic warfare training has been taking place for thousands of years. When God led the Israelites out of Egypt, He needed to prepare them for warfare. When they got to Canaan, they would need to conquer the occupants by military conquest. But they had been *slaves* for 400 years. They were not organized, trained, or equipped for war. Before God would permit them to fight battles, He led Israel out of Egypt into the desert for basic military training. He did not lead them through Philistine country, though that would have been shorter. Here's why:

*"If they face war, they might change their minds and return to Egypt." So God led the people around by the desert road toward the Red Sea. The Israelites went up out of Egypt armed for battle (Exodus 13:17b–18).*

Similarly, the military understands it cannot take people out of civilian life and thrust them into combat. Substantial changes must be made first. Many tasks that soldiers, sailors, and airmen perform in combat have no parallel in civilian life. The military trains each soldier carefully before putting them into combat units. The military's high degree of discipline and unit cohesion must also be acquired. Individualism must be reduced and replaced with a vision of success as a team.

## THE BASICS OF BASIC TRAINING

Most businesses and organizations conduct training for new employees, but nothing compares in scope and purpose to military basic training. The goal of military training is to change the whole individual—a difficult process for the trainer and the trainee! The military intends to change the trainee's attitude, ability, perspective, and values. It aims to make soldiers stronger, smarter, more responsible, more reliable, and more effective than they've ever been.

In a relatively short amount of time (one to four months), an individual is shaped into a soldier on the anvil of basic training. This process has changed little over the centuries. As in a forge, pressure and heat are applied to make the object bend without breaking. Pressures of time, physical activity, mental challenge, and emotional strain are applied simultaneously during basic training for a twofold purpose. The first purpose is to quickly shape the individual into a team member. The second is to "weed out" those who can't stand the pressures of military life. Better to find those people early in training than on a battlefield. The military carefully prescreens recruits and tries to present a candid picture of its requirements to help reduce attrition during basic training. But there is no substitute for real pressure to observe how people respond to stress. New recruits learn their own capacities, and most realize greater capability than they thought they had.

Among the different services, basic training differs in location, length, and technique, but they are alike in the essentials. Officer basic training is often longer because it involves training in leadership as well as military skills. The military academies conduct an initial summer training, lasting a few months, and continue the training for these first-year officer candidates throughout the rest of the year. Regardless of length and location, basic training will emphasize, at the very least, the following elements.

### Physical training

Most military occupations require excellent physical condition. In every job, a healthy, disciplined body increases your ability to accomplish your required duties. The more in shape you are, the better you'll be able to do all that is required in peace and war.

Basic training will introduce you to regular exercise and fitness. Few people will achieve peak physical performance at basic training, but most will progress to a greater level of condition and strength. Physical training adds to the overall stress and fatigue of basic training, which contributes to self-discipline, good time management, and balance. You should arrive at basic training in good physical condition. If you're not in shape, you will struggle with all other areas of the training.

### Military order and discipline

Every service teaches its "basics" to march. Why would this be, when few military units march into battle anymore? Close-order drill has proven an effective tool to teach leadership, teamwork, and self-discipline. In the smallest group of soldiers (called different things in different services), the individual transforms from "me" to "we." Though this seems a small thing, it is the single most important change from life as a civilian. Marching in a group teaches you how to stay in step with others and in line with those in the same column and row. Marching is visual training that demonstrates the precision that can be achieved by individuals working together. You probably won't do much close-order drill after basic training, but you will never forget the life lessons you learn from marching:

➤ What you do must be coordinated with others.

➤ Everyone must obey the leader's voice to succeed.

➤ Some things in life can only be achieved in a group.

You also will learn respect for authority and the importance of obeying orders. While this is a lifelong area of learning, the greatest advance in understanding and adopting these values occurs in basic training. Those who do not internalize these fundamentals will be turned back for additional training or will be discharged.

### Personal grooming and housekeeping

It is a rare person who possesses personal hygiene and house-keeping habits that measure up to military standards. This is one area that changes visibly as you move from civilian to military life. For some, it's also their greatest challenge.

In basic training, individuals from every ethnic, family, and cultural background are placed into closely scrutinized living quarters. Every soldier must conform to precise standards. While this contributes to good health and discipline, it also adds to the overall stress of basic training. Every item of personal grooming and housekeeping is standardized: hair length, personal hygiene, how a bed is made, the arrangement of shoes and clothes in drawers and closets. There is a "right way" for everything. These standards, most of which are actually based on logic, develop a healthy, effective climate in which hundreds of people live together. These habits will train you for the severe conditions you may encounter in the military. They will prepare you to live in the community dormitories, barracks, tents, and ships that will be your home. They also ensure public cleanliness and reduce the risk of disease.

Though there are practical reasons for all of the grooming and housekeeping standards, the principal goal is to build a uniform team capable of doing more as a group than could be achieved as individuals. Individual habits and preferences are shaped to encourage simplicity, cohesion, and uniformity.

## PLAN TO SUCCEED

If you're a new recruit headed to basic training, you may wonder if you can do this. Will it be too hard? Remember that the military's goal is for trainees to complete basic training. Thousands of young men and women successfully complete this training every month. If you arrive in good physical shape and with a positive mental attitude, you will, too. It will be tough. You'll have sore muscles and sleepless nights, and your capacity will be stretched. But you will also share the elation and sense of accomplishment that other graduates feel as you realize how much you have developed in such a short period of time.

## HOW TO PREPARE FOR BASIC TRAINING

No amount of preparation will make basic training easy or fun. But if you understand its process, objectives, and requirements, you will adapt faster and spend more time moving with the current than against it. Here are some tips to help you prepare mentally, physically, emotionally, and spiritually.

➤ **Be in shape.** To succeed in basic training, your body must perform well. Start working out six months in advance. Your preparation should include running, push-ups, pull-ups, and sit-ups, as well as other strength and agility exercises. Run at different times of the day and in different conditions, not just when you are fresh and the weather is ideal. Learn to push yourself beyond what you think you can do. Begin to stretch your capacities now, because that's what basic training is all about.

➤ **Begin molding your personal schedule to military life.** That means getting up early! It's not unusual to begin a training day at 4 A.M. and not get to bed until after 10 P.M. Don't wait for basic training to experience the exhilaration of 4 A.M. wake-ups!

➤ **Talk to others who have been through basic training.** Listen carefully as they share their experiences and feelings. Understand this will be a time of stretching like no other.

➤ **Memorize verses from the Bible that speak of God's presence and help.** Learn them so well that you can recall them easily when you need to. Here are a few you could memorize:

*"So do not fear, for I am with you; do not be dismayed, for I am your God. I will strengthen you and help you; I will uphold you with my righteous right hand" (Isaiah 41:10).*

*I can do everything through him who gives me strength (Philippians 4:13).*

*Consider him who endured such opposition from sinful men, so that you will not grow weary and lose heart (Hebrews 12:3).*

*The LORD is my shepherd, I shall not be in want. He makes me lie down in green pastures, he leads me beside quiet waters, he restores my soul. He guides me in paths of righteousness for his name's sake. Even though I walk through the valley of the shadow of death, I will fear no evil, for you are with me; your rod and your staff, they comfort me. You prepare a table before me in the presence of my enemies. You anoint my head with oil; my cup overflows. Surely goodness and love will follow me all the days of my life, and I will dwell in the house of the LORD forever (Psalm 23).*

Though basic training is not quite the valley of death, it may be the darkest place you have ever walked. Jesus promises to be your Shepherd in every dark valley.

➤ **Develop a sense of humor.** Most aspects of training are serious, but you can find humor in nearly everything. Learning to laugh (preferably to yourself during basic training) makes your days go quickly and frees your mind from the weight of unknown and unreasonable fears.

### A LIFE-CHANGING EXPERIENCE

The days and hours of basic training will be forever etched in your memory. It will be a time of growth, maturing, stretching, and building. You will be expected to adapt to and adopt military values and behavior. Self-centeredness will be aggressively purged, while group success and cooperation will be encouraged. In the end, graduates agree that basic training was challenging, rewarding, and a much-needed first step in becoming a warrior.

*No discipline seems pleasant at the time, but painful. Later on, however, it produces a harvest of righteousness and peace for those who have been trained by it (Hebrews 12:11).*

 **SUMMARY**

⊕ Basic training is where every military person begins military life.

⊕ Basic training will stretch and change you.

⊕ When you enter basic training, be prepared physically, mentally, and spiritually.
⊕ Keep in mind the "big picture" of basic training's purpose—
to shape you into a team member.
⊕ Cooperate with the process and keep your sense of humor.
⊕ If you arrive in good physical shape with a positive attitude,
you will succeed in basic training.

# A Warrior's Work

*Do you see a man skilled in his work? He will serve before kings; he will not serve before obscure men (Proverbs 22:29).*

OUR WORK IS IMPORTANT TO GOD. He gave work to us as a blessing, a source of joy and fulfillment. It also provides the means to support ourselves and our families. The Bible speaks directly about what we do and how we do it. Proverbs 22:29 teaches that a person known for quality work will be placed in positions of increasing trust and responsibility. The quality of our work demonstrates our core values.

A young officer, Captain Wells, diligently accomplished his assigned work. He was accurate, on time, and usually exceeded the expectations of his demanding boss. Captain Wells had been promised a new job, one that he really wanted and would have been good at, but it went to someone else. He remained at his same job, the low man on the totem pole. As a Christian, he had learned to do his best work, regardless of the job, as if he were working for Jesus. Six months later, another position opened. Many people senior to him were eligible for the position, so Captain Wells didn't have much hope in getting the job. But after a week of waiting, he found out he had been selected. His boss was so impressed with his attitude and the quality of his work that he had argued strongly for Captain Wells to be given the new position.

This is a true story, and it happens often. The one who demonstrates faithfulness and quality effort in a smaller, less important job is often rewarded with greater responsibility.

## THE NATURE OF MILITARY WORK

Work itself was not a result of man's fall. It is not a curse. God had assigned work to Adam before he and Eve sinned. The curse of sin brought increased difficulty in work, a resistance that makes the input greater than the output. Once a task is finished, it begins to come apart and decay. Despite this curse, our work provides a sense of accomplishment as we participate with God in taking care of the earth and being stewards of all He has given us. Ecclesiastes 5:12 tells us:

> *The sleep of a laborer is sweet, whether he eats little or much.*

While all work has significance, military work is critically important. Its significance goes beyond individual accomplishment. Together, all of the work military people do results in national security. This is a huge responsibility. Some tasks, like maintaining and using weapons and complex machinery, must be accomplished without a single error, every time. Consider some other critical military jobs:

➤ Launching and recovering aircraft from an aircraft carrier
➤ Assembling a bomb with accurate release settings
➤ Carrying a loaded gun; shooting only at the right target at the right time
➤ Changing components on a nuclear weapon
➤ Loading, aiming, and firing artillery
➤ Analyzing sonar noises and identifying enemy ship noise
➤ Preaching a sermon to soldiers before a battle

This list could fill pages. Every job in the Army, Navy, Air Force, Marines, and Coast Guard involves some measure of danger. Most jobs demand incredibly high levels of accuracy and precision, and most contribute directly to the security and safety of others.

Consider the role an expert sonar technician plays in defending the security of his ship and shipmates. Consider the responsibility of an airborne gunner, who provides defense for the aircraft so the rest of the crew can accomplish the mission. Even the "ordinary" task of the infantry soldier shooting his gun becomes extraordinary when you understand that the precision and skill of each soldier determine the outcome of a battle.

Each job in the military is tightly woven with others. Using lethal force and knowing the enemy is also using lethal force heighten the importance of each person doing his or her job right, the first time, every time. Consider the perspective of another warrior, King David:

*Praise be to the LORD my Rock, who trains my hands for war, my fingers for battle (Psalm 144:1).*

*"With your help I can advance against a troop; with my God I can scale a wall. . . . It is God who arms me with strength and makes my way perfect. He makes my feet like the feet of a deer; he enables me to stand on the heights. He trains my hands for battle; my arms can bend a bow of bronze. You give me your shield of victory; you stoop down to make me great. You broaden the path beneath me, so that my ankles do not turn. I pursued my enemies and crushed them; I did not turn back till they were destroyed. I crushed them completely, and they could not rise; they fell beneath my feet. You armed me with strength for battle; you made*

*my adversaries bow at my feet. You made my enemies turn their backs in flight, and I destroyed my foes"* (2 Samuel 22:30, 33–41).

In these verses, David attributed his ability to make war to God's work in him. Every believer needs to understand this perspective. God gave you abilities when He made you, and He shaped you through your growing-up experiences. You're better at some things than other people are, and you can achieve a higher level of skill in these areas quicker than others. In his autobiography, Air Force pilot Chuck Yeager described his exceptional distance vision. This allowed him to clearly see aircraft at a great distance and identify them as enemy or friendly. This was a "gift" others did not have to the same degree, and it made him a very successful fighter pilot.

All of us have areas of special gifting and exceptional ability. For some, that includes the skills necessary to be a good soldier. The Army has historically selected people who can shoot accurately and consistently to be sharpshooters in sniper regiments. From calibrating critical avionics equipment to launching cruise missiles, every job requires talented and well-trained soldiers, sailors, and airmen.

In the military, the lives of others depend on the accurate and timely performance of required tasks. One of the best examples of this is the coordinated activity during aircraft launch and recovery from an aircraft carrier. Each person on deck wears a colored vest that represents the kind of work they do. Firemen wear one color, positioning directors another, and catapult teams yet another. The crowded and noisy deck holds many groups of people with different tasks. The conditions are tight and dangerous. Stand in the wrong place at the wrong time and you will be injured or killed. Yet every day hundreds of aircraft are launched and recovered from carriers without incident. The safety and success of complex military operations are built on the accurate performance of each task by every person.

Trained soldiers and sailors rise to a level where they can complete tasks under extreme pressure, often in the face of enemy fire. The prophet Joel described the attributes of highly trained and disciplined military units:

> *They charge like warriors; they scale walls like soldiers.*
> *They all march in line, not swerving from their course.*
> *They do not jostle each other; each marches straight*
> *ahead. They plunge through defenses without breaking*
> *ranks (Joel 2:7–8).*

Notice that *each* marches straight ahead, each does what he is trained to do. Yet none jostles another. Their work is done without degrading the work of another. They move as a unit without breaking ranks. The quality of an excellent military unit hinges on these three words: each, all, together.

*Each* one is trained and does his or her job. *All* work at the goal in cooperation with others. *Together* the unit moves and accomplishes its objective. This is true for one unit and for multiple units working together on a battlefield. Each unit must do its work while not interfering with the work of others. Together, the units are able to achieve more than any one of them could alone. History's great campaigns and successful battles all began with each soldier doing his or her duty correctly at the right time.

## MAKING THE MOST OF YOUR WORK

Your work in the military is important—sometimes life-and-death important. In light of this, here are some applications that you, as a Christian soldier, can weave into your work and your life.

➤ **Commit to be *very good* at your assigned tasks.**
This includes not only your primary duties, such as firing a weapon or repairing a component, but also the lesser tasks: cleaning the floor, washing dishes, serving meals, cleaning your equipment, polishing boots.

> *Among all these soldiers there were seven hundred chosen men who were left-handed, each of whom could sling a stone at a hair and not miss (Judges 20:16).*

➤ **Use every resource available to develop your strengths.**
The military will encourage your personal development. You will be given opportunities to increase your skill and learn more. There are also other ways to improve. Recognize that getting better at what you do is your responsibility. Do what you can, on your own, to be the best you can be.

> *"All who are skilled among you are to come and make everything the LORD has commanded" (Exodus 35:10).*

➤ **Work as if Jesus were your direct supervisor.**
It's human nature to work hard and produce high quality only when we are being watched. Unfortunately, this ethic results in faulty work and subpar service. If we knew we would only be paid for perfect production, each task would be done correctly.

Jesus instructs us to work for our earthly boss as if we were working for Him. He also asks us to look to Him for our reward.

> *Whatever you do, work at it with all your heart, as working for the Lord, not for men, since you know that you will receive an inheritance from the Lord as a reward. It is the Lord Christ you are serving (Colossians 3:23–24).*

*Obey them not only to win their favor when their eye is on you, but like slaves of Christ, doing the will of God from your heart. Serve wholeheartedly, as if you were serving the Lord, not men (Ephesians 6:6–7).*

### ➤ Do every task with a good attitude.

Doing everything with a good attitude in the military will "mark" you as being different more than anything else. Over the centuries, soldiers' constant complaining has become proverbial. But God imposes a higher standard on His followers. Your decision to refrain from complaining demonstrates to God and your coworkers that you trust Him to take care of your concerns. With a consistently good attitude, you will contrast with those around you like the stars contrast with the dark sky.

*Do everything without complaining or arguing, so that you may become blameless and pure, children of God without fault in a crooked and depraved generation, in which you shine like stars in the universe (Philippians 2:14–15).*

### ➤ Give a fair day's work for a fair day's wages.

Sergeant Ray worked in the personnel office. A young Christian excited about his new knowledge and experiences, he decided to bring his Bible to work and read it at his desk. He would often read for an hour or more, and sometimes he would share the things he was reading with coworkers. After a few weeks of this, Sergeant Ray's supervisor called him into his office and reprimanded him for squandering government time. At first Sergeant Ray was hurt and figured he was being persecuted for being a Christian. Then a coworker shared this verse with him:

*One who is slack in his work is brother to one who destroys (Proverbs 18:9).*

His friend explained that each person is paid for the work they do. An employer expects to receive a full day of work for a full day of pay. Sergeant Ray began making time during his lunch break and outside of work to read the Bible and also became increasingly skilled at his job. He eventually won honors from his unit.

Zeal for the Lord should not detract from your ability to serve with excellence. On the contrary, your work as a Christian should reflect the high standards you have learned from following Jesus.

*People were overwhelmed with amazement. "He has done everything well," they said (Mark 7:37a).*

Jesus did all things well, and people noticed. We should follow His example.

*Make it your ambition to lead a quiet life, to mind your own business and to work with your hands, just as we told you, so that your daily life may win the respect of outsiders and so that you will not be dependent on anybody (1 Thessalonians 4:11–12).*

➤ **Be loyal in thought, word, and deed.**
The military requires loyalty. It must be thorough and genuine. Seaman Trapper worked as a mess steward aboard ship and frequently served in the officer mess. As he served meals to the officers and overheard their conversations, he formed opinions about people. Sometimes the opinions were his own, but often he learned to like or dislike someone based on the comments he

heard from others. In a conversation with a friend aboard ship, he referred to the captain as "Captain Fearful," a name he had heard others use. Trapper's friend rebuked him. He explained that loyalty involved not only actions but also thoughts and words. Using belittling names for any member of the organization, and especially leaders, hurts the person being criticized, the person speaking, and the whole organization.

*Do not revile the king even in your thoughts, or curse the rich in your bedroom, because a bird of the air may carry your words, and a bird on the wing may report what you say (Ecclesiastes 10:20).*

*A man who lacks judgment derides his neighbor, but a man of understanding holds his tongue (Proverbs 11:12).*

Seaman Trapper and his friend helped each other refrain from criticizing others. When a group of comrades criticized people aboard ship, Trapper and his friend either said nothing or commented positively about the person. Trapper vowed to repeat nothing he heard while serving in his position of trust.

*Reckless words pierce like a sword, but the tongue of the wise brings healing (Proverbs 12:18).*

## YOUR WORK MATTERS

As you serve in the military, give your work the best of your ability and energy. Accuracy and consistency are essential to the fast-paced, often dangerous work required in the military. Additionally, as a Christian, your desire should be to produce quality work that honors God and fulfills the expectations of your supervisors. All work is important, but work in the military is critically important. Your work will impact national security and can potentially affect the millions of lives you have committed to protect.

 **SUMMARY**

⊕ Most military jobs have significance that goes beyond civilian jobs.

⊕ Your work must be of the highest quality all of the time.

⊕ As a Christian, you are to perform to the same high standards whether you're being watched or not.

⊕ Ultimately, you answer to the Lord Jesus for the work you perform.

⊕ What you do with the time and the ability God has given you is a measure of your stewardship and your potential to succeed with increased responsibilities.

# Promotion, Pay, and Contentment

*For promotion cometh neither from the east, nor from the west, nor from the south. But God is the judge (Psalm 75:6–7a, KJV).*

EVERY WALK OF LIFE, EVERY BUSINESS and organization, has structure and hierarchy with senior leaders, mid-level managers, and subordinates. The military did not invent organizational hierarchy, but it did define and refine rank in a way unlike the civilian world. In the military, everyone "wears rank on their sleeve," literally! Rank is also worn on shoulder straps, collars, and hats. Rank in the military is important and prominent. From the most junior enlisted person to the commanding officer, everyone wears rank and understands position in the organization.

Linked directly to rank is pay. The formula, not surprisingly, is very simple. The higher your rank and responsibility, the more you are paid. Power to lead, control, and manage also comes with higher rank. This makes promotion attractive and desirable. Most people want increasing power, authority, and pay. But what should guide a Christian who pursues promotion and greater pay?

It's helpful to incorporate the truth of Psalm 75:6–7 into your thinking about military promotions. God is the judge, the final arbiter, and the eternal master designer. He has a plan for your life. Ultimately, it is God who puts up one and takes down another.

## THE BIBLE SPEAKS TO SOLDIERS

There is not a long list of Bible verses that say specifically, "Military people should do the following . . .", but there is one. We looked at this in Chapter 1. When crowds gathered to hear John the Baptist, he told them, "Produce fruit in keeping with repentance." In other words, he instructed them to live a life on the outside that demonstrated a changed heart. When they asked further, "What should we do?" John answered each group with specifics.

> *Then some* soldiers *asked him, "And* what should we do?" *He replied, "Don't extort money and don't accuse people falsely—be content with your pay"* (Luke 3:14, emphasis added).

This was specific counsel to soldiers on how they should demonstrate a changed heart. The first two commands are against abuse of power. Soldiers carried weapons and wore uniforms that showed their authority came from the State. As armed representatives of the State, they possessed more power than ordinary citizens. When one person possesses more power than another, it can be abused. John told the soldiers if they had repented on the inside, it would show on the outside. Therefore, a soldier who wished to live a righteous life would not abuse the power and authority given to him. How could he abuse it? He could extort money from the people of a conquered nation. He could imprison people on false charges. These practices were fueled by the desire to have more wealth, and they were forbidden by God. Then John capped the soldier's list with this important command: "Be content with your pay."

Imagine some of the other things John could have said: "You soldiers are agents of death. Get out of the military!" But he did not. Instead, he told them to serve honorably, not bending or breaking the rules, and to be content with their pay. These words still hold true today. The military profession is an honorable one, only dishonored by those who abuse their power.

From John's commands, you can take away these principles:

➤ Military service is allowed and honorable.
➤ A soldier can abuse his power.
➤ Greed prompts unethical and illegal behavior.
➤ Soldiers are to be content with their pay.

If you're content with your pay, does this mean you will end up as a "one striper" or a lieutenant? If you have no desire to advance, won't you end up on the bottom rung? Both logic and experience say, "No." Promotion in the military is not based on your ability to sell yourself. It's based on demonstrated ability to perform at the next higher rank. When the military promotes someone, it makes a statement about that person's potential. The U.S. Army created a powerful recruiting slogan, "Be all that you can be!" Your goal should be to fulfill that slogan. Contentment does not mean you shouldn't mature, improve, and be promoted.

Does that mean everyone will rise to the top positions of rank and responsibility? Some will, most will not. For every 100 officers entering the service, only *four* will achieve the rank of colonel. Only a small percentage of colonels will wear a general's star. The reason for this is simple. An army does not need as many colonels as it does lieutenants. It needs fewer majors than captains, fewer still lieutenant colonels. At each increasing rank, it needs fewer people. The same is true for enlisted ranks. By law, only 1 percent of the enlisted force can serve at the top enlisted grade. Think about that as you stand in formation with 100 other people during basic training. Look at the crowd and consider that only a small percent will reach the top ranks.

The military needs a lot of "workers." Ninety percent of the hands-on work is accomplished by men and women in their first enlistment. From among those "first-termers," leadership will pick the best to advance. The rest will either be allowed to remain in the military at their present rank, or they will be released from service at the end of their enlistment.

## A GODLY VIEW OF PROMOTION AND PAY

So what should be your goals for promotion? Here are a few guidelines to remember as you serve in the military:

➤ God created you with specific gifts and abilities.
➤ God is the ultimate "promotion authority."
➤ Promotion will be the result of the work you do and how others evaluate your work.
➤ You can trust the outcome to God.

Your contentment needs to be focused on the character of God. Romans 8:32 (KJV) tells us:

*He that spared not his own Son, but delivered him up for us all, how shall he not with him also freely give us all things?*

This verse does not promise to promote you to the highest rank. It does promise to provide for your needs. For some, He accomplishes His purpose through advancement; for others, He accomplishes it in other ways.

*"For I know the plans I have for you," declares the LORD, "plans to prosper you and not to harm you, plans to give you hope and a future" (Jeremiah 29:11).*

Not being promoted is generally not an indication of incompetence or failure. Many fully qualified people are "passed over" simply because there are not as many senior positions as junior ones. Some are not promoted because He wants to lead them out of the military and on to other work. When God closes a door, He surely opens another somewhere else.

## A BALANCED LIFE

Your objective should be to live a life that reflects balance and trust in God.

> *Therefore, my dear friends, as you have always obeyed— not only in my presence, but now much more in my absence—continue to work out your salvation with fear and trembling, for it is God who works in you to will and to act according to his good purpose (Philippians 2:12–13).*

This passage talks about balance and partnership. Believers are instructed to "work out" their own salvation. That means taking responsibility for your decisions and actions. But this verse is balanced by the following verse. God is working in us according to *His* purpose!

It's good that these two verses are adjacent. If they weren't, some would point to one and overemphasize our responsibility. Others would point to verse 13 and only emphasize God's work. The fact is, responsibility is shared. There is work that you are expected to do, and there are purposes that God accomplishes in you. Apply these verses as you work through the military promotion system. Your responsibility is to do your job to the best of your ability. God's responsibility is to work out the circumstances and events that flow from your work. Do your part and trust God to do His.

> *Do your best to present yourself to God as one approved, a workman who does not need to be ashamed and who correctly handles the word of truth (2 Timothy 2:15).*

This verse instructs us to correctly handle the truth. However, the phrase at the beginning is appropriate in other areas. We are to "do our best." We are to do everything we can to produce quality, timely work.

So what about pay? You may think, "If pay is linked to promotion, I need to be promoted to make more money." This is partly true. But pay raises are also given for time spent in service. In some military specialties, incentives are given for reenlisting and for certain kinds of hazardous work. It is reasonable to expect more pay as your experience and responsibilities increase. But guard your heart against covetousness, jealousy, and greed. The desire to have more money can lead to destructive behavior. The book of 1 Timothy offers this strong warning:

*People who want to get rich fall into temptation and a trap and into many foolish and harmful desires that plunge men into ruin and destruction. For the love of money is a root of all kinds of evil. Some people, eager for money, have wandered from the faith and pierced themselves with many griefs. But you, man of God, flee from all this, and pursue righteousness, godliness, faith, love, endurance and gentleness (1 Timothy 6:9–11).*

The book of Proverbs adds this caution:

*Do not wear yourself out to get rich; have the wisdom to show restraint. Cast but a glance at riches, and they are gone, for they will surely sprout wings and fly off to the sky like an eagle (Proverbs 23:4–5).*

## HARD WORK AND TRUST

Promotion and pay are important aspects of all work. When you pursue them in a balanced way, you will find contentment and fulfillment. If you make them your main focus, you will lose your joy and feel like you never have enough. The military thrives on the system of promoting its most capable people. Strive to be the very best at whatever you do. Trust God to work out the results within the military promotion and pay system. Proverbs 21:1 reminds us that it is easy for Him to move the "king's" heart—that applies to military supervisors and promotion boards, as well.

> *But godliness with contentment is great gain. For we brought nothing into the world, and we can take nothing out of it. But if we have food and clothing, we will be content with that (1 Timothy 6:6–8).*

 **SUMMARY**

⊕ The military, like other organizations, uses a tiered hierarchy.
⊕ Promotion is based on ability, experience, and potential.
⊕ Fewer people are promoted to each higher rank.
⊕ Your responsibility is to be the best you can be.
⊕ We are to be content with our work and pay.
⊕ God rewards your work as He purposes.

# Assignments and Moves

*The LORD had said to Abram, "Leave your country, your people and your father's household and go to the land I will show you" (Genesis 12:1).*

*The LORD replied, "My Presence will go with you, and I will give you rest." Then Moses said to him, "If your Presence does not go with us, do not send us up from here" (Exodus 33:14–15).*

FEW EVENTS IN LIFE ARE MORE STRESSFUL than moving. This was true even in the days of Abram (Abraham) and Moses, both of whom God told to pack their possessions and move. It's comforting—especially when you're in the military—to know that God understands the challenges of moving.

Moving from one place of assignment to another is a prominent feature of military life. If you spend 20 or 30 years in the military, you can plan to make 10 to 20 moves throughout your career. The entire military community is mobile. Even when you are not moving, approximately one-third of your friends and coworkers will be.

This chapter discusses the reason for military moves and your responsibility to help shape assignment decisions. It also addresses the challenges that moving creates.

## THE REASON BEHIND THE MOVES

Why do you have to move? Why can't you stay in one place, at one base, post, or port, for your whole career? It may seem like the military is just trying to test your flexibility, but there are actually several reasons why assignment changes are important and necessary.

### *Worldwide commitment*

The most compelling reason for moves is the U.S. military's involvement overseas. During the past 100 years, the United States has increasingly become a global power, forming alliances, treaties, and partnerships with other nations. The U.S. military sends warriors to places of tension and vital interest throughout the world. Treaties and logistics also determine where military units are positioned. The NATO treaty, in particular, has kept U.S. service members flowing in and out of Europe since World War II.

Most soldiers will serve a "tour" or assignment at an overseas location. These assignments range in length from 12 to 24 months for unaccompanied tours (without family) to 24 to 48 months for accompanied tours. For every soldier, sailor, and airman who goes overseas, another is assigned to fill his or her vacant position stateside. All of this means that between one-third to one-half of the people at a base are on the move at any given time.

### *Increased experience*

Another reason for moving soldiers around is to provide new experiences that increase the breadth and depth of their warfighting skills. The availability of live-fire ranges, for example, determines how much hands-on training you will receive with actual equipment and munitions. Or you may be sent to a new base with more similar terrain and topography to the place you will be deployed.

### Logistics reality

Logistics also shapes assignments. The need for military equipment and personnel can arise quickly and unexpectedly, so some forces are positioned where they respond in a hurry. This concept, called forward positioning, accounts for many of the overseas assignments. The rapid response time required of military units often means they must be placed near potential hot spots throughout the world. Additionally, moving heavy items—fuel, munitions, and equipment—is a very slow process. These items are often positioned in overseas areas before a conflict. People are assigned at these locations to maintain the resources and prepare to transport them when necessary. All of these actions are a military necessity to keep response time to a minimum.

### Improved organizations

The military has embraced the principle that periodic rotation of people encourages change and innovation in the organization. New eyes see challenges and solutions differently. Each successive team of people improves on the work of previous unit members. This keeps people regularly moving in and out of different assignments.

### Personal desires

Some people simply want to change jobs or locations when possible. Service members informally categorize assignments as "best places to serve" and "worst places to serve." Incidentally, this list is not universal. One soldier's "worst" is another soldier's "best." Changing assignments accommodates individual desires with service requirements. The net effect is a better soldier and better unit performance.

For these reasons, the military continues to move people from assignment to assignment. In tight budget years, moves may be made more slowly and assignments may last longer, but this fact remains: If you are in the military for very long, you are going to move.

## GOD GOES WITH YOU

Here is the good news for Christians in the military. Regardless of where you go, how remote the assignment, or how few others are assigned with you, God promises to go with you and to watch over you. Though many things change from assignment to assignment, God's comforting presence and power remain the same no matter where you go. This fact provides a deep sense of comfort and resilience in the face of stressful moves.

Furthermore, the peace you exhibit in the midst of turmoil and change will distinguish you as a Christian and make you a source of comfort to others. It also may lead to opportunities to share your faith with others. Your comrades watch and evaluate how you respond to familiar stress. Your positive attitude will be attractive to the people around you.

> *But in your hearts set apart Christ as Lord. Always be prepared to give an answer to everyone who asks you to give the reason for the hope that you have. But do this with gentleness and respect (1 Peter 3:15).*

## PARTICIPATING IN MILITARY ASSIGNMENTS

Although the military periodically mandates moving, you will have the opportunity to participate in the process. Your active participation will make this aspect of your military experience much more positive.

When it comes to new assignments, individual soldiers have varying degrees of control. In some instances, phase points, or time-in-grade requirements, narrow the window of assignment opportunity. For example, an aircraft crew chief may be required to be an E-5 or E-6 and have at least four years of experience on a certain type of aircraft. It would be impossible to volunteer for this assignment if you did not meet the requirements. Some professional and technical schools are required when you reach a specific number of years or rank. Some assignments have a limited number of billets and a wait list to be assigned to them. Other assignments are "controlled," meaning you're locked into the assignment for three to four years. Many assignments come with rules, requirements, policies, and other factors that are beyond your control. It's important to understand the rules that affect assignment actions within your career field and branch of service.

The flip side is that some assignments are filled primarily by people who volunteer for them. Many have large windows of opportunity (e.g., anytime between 5 and 12 years of service). When there is more flexibility, you will be expected to participate in the assignment process.

The military uses a form, often called a "dream sheet," to facilitate the assignment process. This document is used to submit preferences for geographic location, duty type, overseas preferences, and volunteer statements. This sheet allows you to communicate your "dreams" to the people who write assignments and fill billets. If you could go wherever you wanted and do whatever job you were most qualified for, what would you choose? Your dream sheet should reflect those choices. The closer your "dreams" match the needs of the service, the more likely it is you will get what you request. If you attempt to match your abilities and strengths to what the military needs, the military will work with you to put you in a place and unit that maximizes benefit to both of you. You and the military may completely concur on an assignment action and then both of you benefit. Other times the needs of the organization—and your commitment to defend your country—overrule your individual desires.

Sergeant Brown was approaching the time to move. He had been an exemplary performer in his current unit, and his commander wanted to reward him with the opportunity to choose his next duty assignment. He was told to choose from a list of six possible locations. Sergeant Brown and his wife spent some time discussing and praying about their next assignment, then they wrote out their list in preferred order, from one to six.

The Browns did not know that while they were doing this, the commander was told to assign all of his best out-going personnel to a base that desperately needed qualified people. Before Sergeant Brown could show his commander his list of preferences, the commander apologized because Sergeant Brown was not going to be able to choose his next assignment, after all. The commander had to send him and his family to the base that needed qualified people. An incredible sense of peace flooded over Sergeant Brown. He thanked the commander for his original offer and said he understood that the needs of the military come first. Then he handed him his carefully prayed-over list. His new, required assignment had been his number-one choice!

In addition to jobs within the normal career track, the military has special assignments: honor guard, recruiter, drill instructor, and other kinds of teaching jobs. There are also optional educational and special certification-training assignments. Entry into a special-duty assignment rests almost completely on your own initiative. Occasionally, a supervisor or commander may encourage you to apply for an assignment based on your demonstrated potential, but the decision and application process will be up to you.

Retraining is another important avenue of assignment, and a cooperative decision between you and the service. After a certain period of time, you can request to receive training in a new career field or specialty. Your request will be evaluated based on the needs of the service and vacancies.

This chapter could not possibly describe every assignment possibility and all of the policy variations. But you should be familiar with the different kinds of assignments and your responsibility in the process of job and location selection. You will have little or no input on some assignment decisions and more input on others. Still other assignments will not be made unless you initiate the request. Timing, location, and details of jobs are a result of a partnership between you and the military.

It might seem that the longer you are in the military and the higher your rank, the more say you have in the assignment process. In fact, it often works the other way. People with many years of experience are highly skilled and thoroughly trained. They have demonstrated both technical and leadership aptitude, keeping them on the promotion track. As mentioned in Chapter 5, there are fewer billets in senior ranks than in junior ranks; therefore, senior people have fewer options. Also, some senior officer and NCO billets have special requirements. Laws, which govern specific required qualifications, control others. Taken together, this results in the military having increasing control over a person's assignments as time progresses. Regardless of this, you will still be encouraged to participate in the process.

## A CHRISTIAN'S PERSPECTIVE ON MOVING

The Christian soldier has several promises from God regarding moving. God is omnipotent and has the authority and ability to affect all of your assignments. Humans make assignment decisions, but God can move the hearts and minds of men and women.

*The king's heart is in the hand of the LORD; he directs it like a watercourse wherever he pleases (Proverbs 21:1).*

God can move the heart of a decision-maker just like He can choose to alter the course of a river. Claim this promise each time you enter the "window" of eligibility for a new assignment. Ask God to place you in positions that maximize your skills and training and in locations that will allow you to continue to grow in your relationship with Him.

Consider this verse:

*The lot ["dream sheet"] is cast into the lap, but its every decision is from the* LORD *(Proverbs 16:33).*

Our decisions can be approved or vetoed by the Lord. This does not mean we should not participate in making them. Rather, it gives us greater confidence that after we have done our part in the process, God has the power to confirm or erase the work as it pleases Him. Soldiers in route to an assignment have had their orders changed. Sometimes, the change is baffling or disappointing. Often, we do not understand what God is doing, but you can count on His goodness and His work on your behalf. God cares for you, and He will guide you.

*He who did not spare his own Son, but gave him up for us all—how will he not also, along with him, graciously give us all things? (Romans 8:32).*

Assignments and moves stretch your faith and build your trust in the sovereignty of God. He can use this unique feature of military life to show Himself strong in your life.

*For the eyes of the* LORD *run to and fro throughout the whole earth, to show himself strong in the behalf of them whose heart is perfect toward him (2 Chronicles 16:9a, KJV).*

## CHALLENGES

Though you participate in the assignment process and trust

God to lead you, new assignments will still bring challenges. Each new location and job can stretch your skills, attitude, and faith. These are some of the specific challenges you may face.

➤ **Being away from home.** You will probably be asked to move away from your extended family, your support system, and all that is familiar to you. In fact, the concept of "home" is a little different for military people than for civilians. If you ask career military people where they are *from*, a common answer is, "I'm in the military; I'm from all over." While in the military, most men and women learn to operate without the support of extended family members and a familiar community.

➤ **Economic stress.** Moving can be expensive, and all expenses are not always reimbursed. Economic stress can also lead to marital and family tension.

➤ **Loss of friendships.** When you realize that one-third of the people you know will move by the end of the year, you're forced to make quick friendships. You'll also lose close contact with your friends each time you move.

➤ **Disruption of fellowship and accountability.** Christians depend on fellowship with other believers to encourage, build up, and pray for the needs of one another. It takes a long time to develop the kind of trust and support necessary for a healthy accountability relationship. These relationships are not quickly replaced at the new assignment.

➤ **Assignment to an undesirable location or job.** Foreign and unfamiliar assignments can be especially challenging to soldiers and their families. Some assignments cause family separation, creating stress and hardships at home. Sometimes the location is fine, but the particular job may require extended on-duty time or frequent travel away from the family or familiar support group.

> **Disruption of education.** Military people involved in off-duty education are sometimes relocated in the middle of a semester or degree program. Sometimes credits are not transferable to a new location.

## MEETING THE CHALLENGES

Prior planning can provide solutions to most of these challenges. Compensate for family separation by developing new friendships and support relationships with other military and community people. Set aside money ahead of time for upcoming moves to relieve your economic stress. Research churches and other fellowship opportunities at your new location before you arrive there so you can get connected faster. Remember that assignments to less desirable places can turn out, surprisingly, to be among your very best.

Major Goodman received an assignment to one of those "less desirable" places. He realized, as a Christian, that God had not fallen asleep and let his assignment slip through accidentally. He began to pray and seek wisdom on how to make the best of the assignment. Shortly after his arrival, the first of five major storms rolled in from the sea, devastating much of the island on which his family lived. The community and base personnel set up action committees to respond to the disasters. In the process, Major Goodman's family formed some deep friendships that lasted years after this assignment ended. His family also became closer as they began to see the humor in all of the stresses they endured together. Years later, when asked about that assignment, each family member gave reasons why it had been one of their best experiences.

## THE BRIGHT SIDE OF MOVING

The challenges and realities of multiple moves might lead you to believe that this is the worst part of military service. However, for many service members, moving to new locations and making new friends are the best parts of being in the military. Whether each new assignment becomes your best or worst depends almost entirely on your own decisions, attitude, and adaptability.

After years of moving and establishing new relationships, some military people actually suffer from *withdrawal* when they leave the military and settle in one place. The experience of moving, change, and challenge becomes an acceptable—even enjoyable—part of military life for these people.

Being aware of the adventures and challenges will prepare you for the reality of the nomadic military lifestyle. God promises to be present in every detail of the process. Regardless of the assignment location, timing, or living arrangements, He will guide you and be with you. He promises that, through His power in you, you will be able to do what He asks. In seeking His will, His involvement, and His strength, you will mature and become convinced that God is worthy of your trust.

> *"When you pass through the waters,* I will be with you; *and when you pass through the rivers, they will not sweep over you. When you walk through the fire, you will not be burned; the flames will not set you ablaze. For I am the* LORD, *your God, the Holy One of Israel, your Savior"* (Isaiah 43:2–3a, emphasis added).

 **SUMMARY**

⊕ In the military, you can expect to move, on average, every three years.

⊕ The military has good reasons for requiring its people to move. Learn about them and understand them.

⊕ You will be able to participate in the process of choosing many assignments.

⊕ Moving is an opportunity to experience God's care for you.

CHAPTER 7

# Professional Development

*And the boy Samuel continued to grow in stature and in
favor with the LORD and with men (1 Samuel 2:26).*

MANY PEOPLE ENTER THE MILITARY, serve for a few years,
and then return to civilian life. While in the military, they develop
self-discipline, maturity, character, and the technical skills and
experience they will use to adapt easily to civilian jobs. Although
it is a good experience and a foundation for their future, these
one-term soldiers don't make the military a lifelong career.

Others, on the other hand, enter the military fully intending
to serve only one term but are attracted to the *espirit de corps,*
discipline, camaraderie, and the military way of life. At the end
of their initial commitment, they realize the military suits them
and that their skills and abilities are a good match for the military. Military service becomes more than a job or a paycheck—
it becomes a profession, a way of life. This group continues in
the military, comprising the core of professional soldiers,
sailors, and airmen who train and lead the rest of the force.

Healthy organizations need committed and experienced
leaders, and the military is no exception. Each year, the armed
services evaluate their people and search for those who demonstrate potential for increased responsibility and a higher capacity to lead. Selection is based on past performance, attitude,
character, talent, and potential.

*"His master replied, 'Well done, good and faithful servant! You have been faithful with a few things; I will put you in charge of many things. Come and share your master's happiness!' " (Matthew 25:21).*

This familiar New Testament verse illustrates the process of evaluation and selection. Like the master in this story, the military is looking for individuals who have been faithful with smaller responsibilities. To those who have demonstrated faithfulness, self-discipline, and leadership potential, the military offers increased rank and responsibility.

## TO CONTINUE OR NOT

The decision to make a career of the military is an important one, made by both the soldier and the military. If each agrees that further service is beneficial, they enter into a contract for additional training and service.

As a Christian, you should make this decision a matter of prayer. Counsel from others is also extremely valuable. At a minimum, this would include feedback from supervisors and frank discussions with peers and family members. It's also wise to seek the counsel of other career military people. And of course, if you are married, be sure your spouse is in agreement. To make your decision, consider your personal strengths and goals and the advice you've received from counselors and from God's Word. Only then will you be able to proceed on this course with unwavering commitment.

## LEADERSHIP TRAINING

If you are willing to spend additional years serving your country, the military will increase its commitment to you. You can expect to receive additional training in your skill area, as well as leadership and management. At every level, military units thrive on good leadership. For this reason, all branches of service have developed an extensive, multitiered curriculum of professional education and leadership training. The timing and course content vary among services, but much is similar.

### Initial training

The first level of leadership school is targeted to soldiers with three to four years of experience. This school teaches "followership" as a prerequisite to leadership, because effective leaders were once loyal followers. Here the students learn about loyalty, innovation, enthusiasm, and other behaviors and attitudes that contribute to a healthy organization. These schools reinforce values introduced in basic training, such as integrity, physical and mental stamina, and personal responsibility. Although some of these courses are taught in a traditional classroom, much of the training is done through activities, such as sports, group problem-solving workshops, close-order drill, and obstacle or confidence courses. The out-of-classroom activities serve as leadership laboratories in which students experiment with leadership styles and methods of communication. As students participate in activities, they analyze their own performance and that of others, learning the importance of evaluation and feedback.

Many of the services employ the "Project X" concept. This is a series of staged scenarios in which certain equipment is provided to accomplish a timed task. Some students are assigned to develop a workable plan and execute it within the allotted time. Others are assigned to evaluate communication, risk taking, adaptation, response to setbacks, listening skills, and overall success. After each task is concluded, everyone participates in an on-the-spot feedback session.

The first tier of leadership training is usually mandatory for all service members. It prepares young officers and enlisted men and women for beginning leadership responsibilities and serves as an evaluation tool, identifying those with potential for additional rank and authority.

### Advanced training

A smaller number of soldiers are then sent to the second tier of training schools. These are phased with other assignments and duties and occur every six to eight years, with each becoming increasingly rigorous. The highest level of officer and enlisted Professional Military Education (PME) is reserved for a select group, identified as the best in that branch of service. At this level, the different branches exchange students and faculty to broaden their own people.

Each of the services has its own course arrangement, structure, and duration. However, they are similar in most of these ways:

➤ Officers and enlisted personnel are expected to complete all levels of PME as they advance. Individuals are expected to complete appropriate levels of PME to be considered for further promotion.

➤ This training has three to four levels, spaced at approximately every four years.

➤ Schools become increasingly longer. The top school usually lasts 3 to 10 months.

➤ Each successive school selects fewer people to attend in residence. Resident schools are highly selective based on past performance and potential.

➤ Those who are not selected to attend in residence are expected to complete the written coursework by correspondence or in seminar at their own duty location.

➤ Schools transition from more emphasis on laboratory and physical activities to more classroom and research activities.

➤ Speaking and writing skills receive more emphasis at higher-level schools.

➤ The goal of all the schools is to develop capable leaders who can think, relate to people, write, speak, and develop appropriate courses of action in any situation.

As you move to higher-level courses, the objectives broaden from military subjects to discussions of national policy and international relations. Students transition from understanding lower-level capability (such as organization and tactics) to national objectives and strategy. Each level continues to teach history, doctrine, and traditions of its own service while exposing its members to some of that information about the other services.

In the upper-level course, students are required to do original research to increase their understanding of their profession (e.g., the role of technology in warfare, the lessons of history, the purpose and effectiveness of alliances). Many of the professional military-education schools incorporate wargaming and thought-provoking exercises to prepare students for wartime responsibilities. The services continue to tailor and shape their professional military-education programs to current world situations, resulting in exceptionally well-prepared warriors.

## JOB-SPECIFIC TRAINING

In addition to PME, the services require advanced training in core skills for career soldiers, such as advanced avionics, weapons engineering, advanced tactics, and principles of logistics support. This training is provided through resident classes and correspondence courses. Through all of these steps, training records are documented to ensure that emerging warriors have completed all assigned training and have demonstrated the capability to accomplish their required tasks. Many senior soldiers become the trainers and certifying officials for new recruits and trainees. The goal of the specific job-related courses is to ensure the military is composed of experts in every area of combat and support.

## TRAINING ON YOUR OWN

If you choose to continue in the military, you are responsible to progress in your technical, managerial, and leadership skills. In addition to the training provided by the military, you will be required to continue to develop your mind, body, and skills on your own. This includes physical conditioning, reading books and articles that increase your professional knowledge, and developing a growing sense of pride in the service and responsibility for its accomplishments.

Expect to be regularly evaluated for leadership capability. In every group, whether among mechanics, computer operators, or riflemen, the military needs excellent leaders. The ability to motivate, communicate, and guide groups of people is an art. Those who demonstrate desire and capacity in these areas are promoted to higher levels.

## "UP OR OUT"

From its investment in the individual soldier, the military expects a return on its time and money.

*"From everyone who has been given much, much will be demanded; and from the one who has been entrusted with much, much more will be asked" (Luke 12:48b).*

Soldiers who want to continue in the military must show progress and growth commensurate with their years of experience. The U.S. military employs an "up or out" personnel system. This means you will be encouraged to progress in rank and ability. Soldiers are kept on active duty based on the level of rank they have attained; lower ranks are allowed to stay fewer years.

This keeps the military thriving and provides opportunity for emerging leaders to fill key positions.

The goal of the military is to select a small group of the most skilled and talented men and women to lead, select, and train future generations of leaders and warriors. Consider these groups from among King David's warriors.

*These were the men who came to David at Ziklag, while he was banished from the presence of Saul son of Kish (they were among the warriors who helped him in battle; they were armed with bows and were able to shoot arrows or to sling stones right-handed or left-handed; they were kinsmen of Saul from the tribe of Benjamin):*
*. . . men of Issachar, who understood the times and knew what Israel should do—200 chiefs, with all their relatives under their command; men of Zebulun, experienced soldiers prepared for battle with every type of weapon, to help David with undivided loyalty—50,000 (1 Chronicles 12:1-2, 32-33, emphasis added).*

Little has changed over the centuries. David was looking for skilled warriors. He needed good fighters and men "who understood the times and knew what to do." These men became the officers in David's army.

If you want to make a career of the military, you must understand the expectation for continuous personal development and lifelong technical and professional growth. You will be evaluated continually and compared with your peers. The best will be selected for increased rank and responsibility. To those to whom much is given, much will be demanded.

*Endure hardship with us like a good soldier of Christ Jesus. No one serving as a soldier gets involved in civilian affairs—he wants to please his commanding officer. Similarly, if anyone competes as an athlete, he does not receive the victor's crown unless he competes according to the rules. Reflect on what I am saying, for the Lord will give you insight into all this (2 Timothy 2:3–5, 7).*

A parallel passage, which speaks of spiritual growth and development, is found in 1 Thessalonians:

*Finally, brothers, we instructed you how to live in order to please God, as in fact you are living. Now we ask you and urge you in the Lord Jesus to do this more and more (1 Thessalonians 4:1, emphasis added).*

Professional development in the military centers on doing the right things "more and more." The military needs people who learn lessons at one level and can easily adapt those lessons to the next level of responsibility. Through this process, the "new guys" mature, learn the ropes, and become the next generation of leaders.

 **SUMMARY**

⊕ Professional development focuses on building greater depth in skills and knowledge.

⊕ Advancement in rank and authority is linked to completing professional training.

⊕ Continuing training includes advanced courses in specific skill areas, as well as leadership and communications.

⊕ In-residence courses are highly selective and depend on your daily performance and attitude.

⊕ The goal of all PME is to make you the very best in a profession in which being second-best is unacceptable.

# Part II:
# The Fruitful Christian Life

IF YOU DIDN'T KNOW IT BEFORE, by now it's clear: Military life is very different from civilian life. And it should be, given the very serious mission that the military undertakes.

So how does your relationship with Christ fit into this demanding life? Is it possible to be both a quality soldier and a dedicated Christian? Absolutely! Building on the information in Part I, the next seven chapters introduce the idea of effectively integrating the principles of Christ's teaching with a highly demanding job in the military. We'll start by looking at the basics of the fruitful Christian life and then move on to consider how these affect your relationships with others.

If you want to be effective and fruitful as a Christian in the military, you must strive to be highly competent at your military skill and credible and consistent in your walk with Christ. This section will provide insight to make that happen.

# A Vital Relationship with God

*"I am the vine; you are the branches. If a man remains in me and I in him, he will bear much fruit; apart from me you can do nothing. . . . This is to my Father's glory, that you bear much fruit, showing yourselves to be my disciples" (John 15:5, 8).*

*Whoever claims to live in him must walk as Jesus did (1 John 2:6).*

GOD LOVES ALL OF HIS CREATED BEINGS, and He wants to have a vital, life-giving relationship with each of them. He desires to be the Lord on the throne of every life—the position to which He has rightful claim. He created us, He gifted us, and through Jesus Christ, He opened the way into His presence. But He does not *make us* yield to His invitation. He woos us, He speaks to our hearts, and He provides for our daily needs. Yet He does not force us to follow Him. We can choose to accept or refuse all He offers.

How do you know if you are "saved" or "born again"? Perhaps the clearest answer comes from Jesus Himself:

*"I tell you the truth, whoever hears my word and believes him who sent me has eternal life and will not be condemned; he has crossed over from death to life" (John 5:24).*

Eternal salvation comes when you accept the free gift of God, by faith, and when you receive forgiveness for your sin based on Jesus' death on the cross. Then you receive the Holy Spirit as the down payment on your eternal life. As a Christian, you are then instructed to go out into the world and live in a way that causes others to see the life of Jesus in all you say and do.

If you have never taken this first step—receiving the free gift of salvation through faith in the work of Jesus—consider doing it now. Talk it over with a Christian friend or pastor and ask them to pray with you. If you have made this commitment but have not matured much in your faith, this chapter points the way to spiritual growth.

A vital personal relationship with God is the most important part of the Christian life. We must either choose to live "plugged in" to God and His resources or choose to go our own way. Ephesians 2:10 declares that "we are God's workmanship, created in Christ Jesus to do good works." This does not mean, as many assume, that we work our way into God's affection or that our good works "earn" His love. Rather, it means that as His followers, we were created and saved so we could participate with God in His work. When we invite Him into our life, He forgives our sin and opens the way to a vital relationship with Him. As with all relationships, it takes time every day to develop a living and active relationship with God.

In all Christians, Christ is *present*. In many, He is *prominent*; in a smaller number, He is *preeminent*. You can tell that those in this latter group are connected to the Vine—Jesus—because of the "fruit" in their lives. (In biblical terminology, "fruit" includes godly character, good works, and leading others to Christ.) You sense holiness that comes from their closeness to God. When they speak, you hear God's truth. Their character reminds you of Jesus.

What would it take for Jesus to be preeminent in your life? What does it mean to be continuously connected to the Vine? That's what we'll look at in this chapter.

## MAINTAINING A RELATIONSHIP WITH GOD

God asks us to make three commitments in order to stay closely connected to Him:

➤ Love God.
➤ Talk to God.
➤ Obey God's Word.

### *Love God*

> *Hear, O Israel: The LORD our God, the LORD is one. Love the LORD your God with all your heart and with all your soul and with all your strength (Deuteronomy 6:4–5).*

Above all else, we are to love God. Throughout this chapter, we will look at activities and practices that help us develop a vital relationship with God. However, activities are not a substitute for loving God. Our love for God is the fuel that powers the activities. In the book of Deuteronomy, God commanded us to love Him with all our heart, soul, and strength, not just the "religious" part of us. Jesus reiterated this, calling it the greatest of all God's commandments.

> *"Love the Lord your God with all your heart and with all your soul and with all your mind and with all your strength" (Mark 12:30).*

If we do not love God with our entire being—*heart, soul, mind, and strength*—we'll have weak areas in our relationship with Him. These weak areas may tempt us to stray and ignore God's leading in our lives. Our allegiance to Him must be absolute. If God is not Lord *of all*, He is not Lord at all! Our love for Him should not be forced or constrained; it should come naturally. If we consider all God has done for us, it's not hard to love Him in return.

*And so we know and rely on the love God has for us. God
is love. Whoever lives in love lives in God, and God in him.
. . . We love because he first loved us (1 John 4:16, 19).*

Loving God is a choice of our will. Our love for Him should
grow daily as we spend time with Him and get to know Him
more. There is no substitute for loving God—not sharing the
Gospel, not leading people to Christ, not religious activity, not
lengthy time in prayer. These activities flow out of a love relationship with God. No activity and no person should have the
place of affection in our souls that is God's. Ask yourself, "Do I
love God with all of my heart, soul, strength, and mind? Is there
evidence of this in the way I live, use my time, treat others, and
establish priorities?" Take time each week to ask yourself, "Do I
love God, and does my life reflect it?"

*I love the LORD, for he heard my voice; he heard my cry for
mercy (Psalm 116:1).*

### Talk to God

*Do not be anxious about anything, but in everything, by
prayer and petition, with thanksgiving, present your
requests to God. And the peace of God, which tran-
scends all understanding, will guard your hearts and
your minds in Christ Jesus (Philippians 4:6–7, emphasis
added).*

*"This, then, is how you should pray: 'Our Father in
heaven, hallowed be your name, your kingdom come,
your will be done on earth as it is in heaven. Give us
today our daily bread. Forgive us our debts, as we also
have forgiven our debtors. And lead us not into temptation, but deliver us from the evil one'" (Matthew 6:9–13).*

When we love someone, we want to talk to them. We want to share what's in our heart and on our mind. Prayer is our opportunity to communicate with God. It's more than just "asking for stuff." Rather, it is the time when we humbly approach God and share our heart with Him. We talk to Him about the issues in our lives and seek His guidance, wisdom, and assurance. It's also a time when we seek His will and ask Him to meet our needs as only He can. Like the other facets of our relationship with God, this is a growing discipline. Our prayer life will not reach a final destination; it is a continuous journey.

You may wonder about the specifics of prayer—when you should pray, where you should pray, and what you should pray about. There are no precise, universal answers to these questions. Imagine you have just gotten married, and ask yourself the same questions with regard to your mate: "When should we talk, where should we talk, what should we talk about?" It sounds pretty silly, doesn't it? You would want to talk to your new life-partner as much as you could, everywhere and about everything. You would want to listen to him or her, as well, to learn more about this person you love so much. The example of marriage is a good one. In the Bible, God uses the picture of marriage to describe our relationship with Christ. We should get to know our Savior and Lord and learn more about Him each day.

Jesus' life and actions establish a pattern for when and where we should talk to God.

*Very early in the morning, while it was still dark, Jesus got up, left the house and went off to a solitary place, where he prayed (Mark 1:35).*

Why did Jesus get up very early? He knew He had a busy day ahead of Him, and He wanted to begin it with His Father. He went someplace where He could be alone. Why? He did not want to be interrupted, and He considered prayer a private activity. Jesus said this about prayer:

*"But when you pray, go into your room, close the door and pray to your Father, who is unseen. Then your Father, who sees what is done in secret, will reward you" (Matthew 6:6).*

So how is this possible for someone in the military? Military people already begin their day very early. Some are awake and at work when the sun rises. You might argue, "Jesus could control His own schedule; in the military I rarely have that luxury."

It's true, Jesus seemed to have more control over His own schedule. But that was not always the case. The verses preceding Mark 1:35 tell us that Jesus worked well into the night, healing many people with diseases. He still managed to get up early and begin his day in prayer. By His life, Jesus demonstrated that prayer was a priority.

If you work swing shift (1600–2400), your day may begin when you get up in the morning. If you work mid-shift (midnight–0800), your day may begin at noon or later, after you have slept. Regardless of when you work, the principle remains the same. Set aside part of your first available waking time to fellowship with God.

Finding a solitary place may also be a challenge. The solitary place Jesus found did not remain that way for long. Peter and the other disciples soon found Jesus, interrupting His solitude. Sometimes the only place available to you will be your bed. You may have to pull the blanket over your head to spend your first waking moments talking to God. The discipline of daily time alone with God can be maintained in the military, but it takes commitment, creativity, and flexibility.

We see this in the Bible through Daniel's commitment to

prayer. Despite a decree forbidding prayer to God, he continued his normal practice, praying to God three times a day.

> *Now when Daniel learned that the decree had been published, he went home to his upstairs room where the windows opened toward Jerusalem. Three times a day he got down on his knees and prayed, giving thanks to his God, just as he had done before (Daniel 6:10).*

Sometimes you'll have to change your habits and schedule out of military necessity. Sometimes your "quiet place" will not be so quiet. You may be so frustrated that you're tempted to end your habit of prayer. Don't stop! Adjust. Alter your schedule. Seek out a new place, but don't quit praying!

Here are the essentials of a vital prayer life:
➤ We pray to God because we love Him and want to talk to Him.
➤ Prayer is a daily priority. We give God our first and best time.
➤ There will be opposition to prayer; continue anyway.
➤ Prayer is private. Find a quiet and solitary place when possible.

> *Then Jesus told his disciples a parable to show them that they should always pray and not give up (Luke 18:1).*

### Obey God's Word

> *All Scripture is God-breathed and is useful for teaching, rebuking, correcting and training in righteousness, so that the man of God may be thoroughly equipped for every good work (2 Timothy 3:16–17).*

> *Jesus answered, "It is written: 'Man does not live on bread alone, but on every word that comes from the mouth of God'" (Matthew 4:4, emphasis added).*

God has spoken to humans. His words are recorded in the Bible. Most, if not all, of what we need to know about life and our relationship with our Father is written down for us to read. Jesus emphasized the importance of every word that comes from the mouth of God. *Every word!* The practice of reading the Bible is as important to our souls as eating is to our bodies. The book of Job states it this way:

> *"I have not departed from the commands of his lips; I have treasured the words of his mouth more than my daily bread" (Job 23:12, emphasis added).*

For Job, God's words were more important than even his food. Try this little experiment some time. Make a commitment to not eat anything each day until you have spent 10 minutes reading the Bible. Do that for one week. Jot down a few notes each day to record your thoughts through the week. At the end of the week, you will have lived out the principle Job expressed. You will have given God's Word first priority.

Think about what currently gets done in a day of your life. Those are your priorities. Are you spending time each day reading the Word of God? If not, it is not a priority in your life. Pick a time in your schedule and begin the practice of daily Bible reading. Initially, it will be a struggle. Building good habits always is. The entire Bible (every word!) can be read in one year by reading three chapters a day. That takes about 15 minutes each day.

God wants us to know His Word. Each page of the Bible contains important, relevant truth for living. In the Ephesians 6 description of the armor of God, the Word of God is called a sword. It is the only piece listed that can be used for offense. A Christian who does not know the Word of God has no offensive capability. Read through Psalm 119. This whole chapter (the longest one in the Bible) describes the value of God's Word and how to use it.

When you joined the military, you were issued a variety of clothing and equipment. God gives you everything you need in one piece of "equipment," the Bible. It's your food, weapon, clothing, light, and compass. But you must become adept at using this valuable piece of equipment. Imagine being issued a military weapon and not using it until the first time you needed it in combat! Paul charged Timothy with this command:

> *Do your best to present yourself to God as one approved, a workman who does not need to be ashamed and who correctly handles the word of truth (2 Timothy 2:15).*

Reading the Bible every day is essential to maintaining a vital relationship with God. It will equip you for every work that you do in the spiritual realm. It also prepares you to respond to every issue you face in the natural world.

One of the most useful and practical books of the Bible is Proverbs, found right in the middle of most Bibles. Since Proverbs contains 31 chapters, it works out well to read one chapter each day. The chapters are packed with practical wisdom for every situation you will face. Every soldier, sailor, and airman needs to have a working knowledge of Proverbs. Here's how the book begins:

> *The proverbs of Solomon son of David, king of Israel: for attaining wisdom and discipline; for understanding words of insight; for acquiring a disciplined and prudent life, doing what is right and just and fair; for giving prudence to the simple, knowledge and discretion to the young (Proverbs 1:1–4).*

These amazing claims are very relevant to your life in the military! Proverbs is an important book for understanding life issues and for gaining a growing measure of wisdom.

One final thought on the value of God's Word to the military person: When General Joshua was about to begin the military campaign to conquer Canaan, God met and instructed him. He said Joshua's success would be linked to obedience to God's Word. He instructed Joshua to meditate day and night on God's Word so he would know it and obey it. God's command to Joshua is as valid for modern warriors as it was for ancient ones. The warrior's life is a demanding one, often filled with life-and-death decisions. The Bible provides the "moral compass" and necessary instructions for every walk of life, including the military.

> *"Do not let this Book of the Law depart from your mouth; meditate on it day and night, so that you may be careful to do everything written in it. Then you will be prosperous and successful" (Joshua 1:8).*

### DAILY QUIET TIME

The practices of reading and meditating on the Word of God, coupled with time in prayer, are called a quiet time or devotional time. It can also include a time of thanksgiving and praise. The vitality of your Christian life will be directly proportional to the consistency of your quiet time in the presence of God. The more time you spend with Him—in His Word, in prayer, in praise— the more you will understand His character and become like Him. The deeper your abiding relationship, the greater your victory and fruitfulness.

> *Then, because so many people were coming and going that they did not even have a chance to eat, he said to*

*them,* "Come with me by yourselves to a quiet place *and get some rest." So they went away by themselves in a boat to a solitary place (Mark 6:31–32, emphasis added).*

*When they saw the courage of Peter and John and realized that they were unschooled, ordinary men, they were astonished and they took note that these men had been with Jesus (Acts 4:13).*

### CHANGED, EQUIPPED, AND SUSTAINED

Spending time with Jesus in our devotional time will change us. Knowing the Bible well will equip us. Loving God with all our heart, mind, strength, and soul will sustain the habits and disciplines of our Christian life and help us maintain a vital, growing relationship with God.

 **SUMMARY**

⊕ A vital relationship with God is essential to a fruitful, victorious Christian life.
⊕ Three commitments will help you establish this relationship: love God, talk to God, and obey God's Word.
⊕ Daily time spent praying and reading the Bible will take you deeper in your relationship with God.
⊕ Start your day with God's words of wisdom and truth. Make your first thoughts His.
⊕ Having a consistent daily quiet time takes discipline, but it is the bedrock upon which all Christian character and service are formed.

# Evangelism

*"Do you not say, 'Four months more and then the harvest'? I tell you, open your eyes and look at the fields! They are ripe for harvest" (John 4:35).*

GOD HAS CHOSEN TO SPREAD the Gospel *through people*. He entrusts ordinary human beings with the privilege and responsibility to reach out to the world with the message of eternal salvation. At the end of Matthew's gospel, we find Jesus' Great Commission to His disciples:

*Then Jesus came to them and said, "All authority in heaven and on earth has been given to me. Therefore go and make disciples of all nations, baptizing them in the name of the Father and of the Son and of the Holy Spirit, and teaching them to obey everything I have commanded you. And surely I am with you always, to the very end of the age" (Matthew 28:18–20).*

All four of the gospel writers record this command, Jesus' last while He was on earth. The writer of Psalm 107:2 indicates that those whom the Lord has redeemed are to *say so*. When God saves someone from sin, He wants that person to be part of the process of saving another. Every Christian has the privilege and responsibility to share the Gospel with others.

## COMMUNICATING THE GOSPEL

We communicate the truth of salvation to the world around us in two ways. One is through our actions; the other is by our words. Both are important. We cannot expect to lead someone to faith in Jesus with our words if our life does not match what we say. Conversely, we cannot expect someone to understand the Gospel simply by observing our life. Jesus has made it possible for us to live victorious and pure lives, but we must also explain His message and the effect He has had on us. As we walk closely with Christ, we should always be prepared to tell why we live the way we do.

> *But in your hearts set apart Christ as Lord. Always be prepared to give an answer to everyone who asks you to give the reason for the hope that you have. But do this with gentleness and respect (1 Peter 3:15).*

### *Our actions*

> *"You are the light of the world. A city on a hill cannot be hidden. Neither do people light a lamp and put it under a bowl. Instead they put it on its stand, and it gives light to everyone in the house. In the same way,* let your light shine before men, *that they may see your good deeds and praise your Father in heaven" (Matthew 5:14–16, emphasis added).*

Our lives are to be light to the world. Our conduct as Christians should be patterned after the life of Jesus. In the book of 1 John, the author wrote: "Whoever claims to live in him *must walk as Jesus did*" (1 John 2:6, emphasis added). That is a high standard, but it's what Jesus asks of those who claim Him as Lord. In what areas of our life might others observe "light" in us?

➤ **Our work.** Every day, people watch what we do on the job and how we do it. Work as if Jesus is right by your side and you're trying to please Him. (See Chapter 4 for more on this.)

➤ **Our moral behavior.** God has called us to be holy. Our honest, honorable behavior is the mark of a follower of Jesus, setting us apart from the world around us. (Read more on this in Chapter 17.)

➤ **The way we treat people.** When the Golden Rule is operative in our life, others will take notice. It is a rare person who treats everyone with courtesy and respect. When we do, we give powerful testimony for Jesus.

➤ **The way we think.** The basis for our thinking should be the truth as revealed in God's Word. We ought to reflect confidence in knowing how to make good decisions, and we should demonstrate godly wisdom in our speech and actions.

➤ **Our words.** At all times—not just when we share our faith—our speech should be pure, edifying, and encouraging. Nothing reveals the heart as much as a person's words.

When we allow the Holy Spirit to dwell in us and control our life, we offer light to the world. A life that gives light is attractive. It causes others to wonder why we are different. It often earns us the privilege of sharing the Gospel with others. Always, though, we must realize that our lives alone do not communicate the whole Gospel; our words are just as important.

### Our words

*Simon Peter answered him, "Lord, to whom shall we go? You have the words of eternal life" (John 6:68, emphasis added).*

*"For I did not speak of my own accord, but the Father who sent me commanded me what to say and how to say it. I know that his command leads to eternal life. So what-*

*ever I say is just what the Father has told me to say"*
*(John 12:49–50, emphasis added).*

The Gospel is not merely a nice set of principles. It's not just another way to think about life or one of many possible roads to God. Both Peter and Jesus tell us that the Gospel contains *the only way* to eternal life! It is the way that can save human beings from the penalty and punishment for sin, but salvation through Christ is not a human idea. It was conceived wholly in the mind of God. And for men and women to consider the message of the Gospel, they've got to hear it! For them to hear it, someone must share it.

The military requires ID cards and vehicle stickers to get onto bases, posts, ports, and ships. Because the military is a relatively closed environment, the traveling evangelist or the local pastor does not have easy access to this community. "Insiders"—Christians in the military—have the best opportunity to share the Gospel in this environment.

Here are some of the ways you could share with your coworkers:

➤ **Your testimony.** Tell how you came to hear and understand the Gospel and what difference it made in your life.

*"For we cannot help speaking about what we have seen and heard" (Acts 4:20).*

➤ **A short Gospel presentation.** Be able to communicate the main points of the Gospel, using Bible verses. Prepare and practice beforehand.

*Pray also for me, that whenever I open my mouth, words may be given me so that I will fearlessly make known the mystery of the gospel (Ephesians 6:19).*

➤ **Other pertinent verses from God's Word.** You will probably be involved in conversations about subjects the Bible clearly addresses. In the context of your day-to-day conversations, learn to become comfortable sharing what the Bible says about life issues. Not every discussion allows for a full presentation of the Gospel, but many times you can share a few relevant verses of God's wisdom. Those conversations will often lead to other opportunities to share the whole Gospel.

*Preach the Word; be prepared in season and out of season; correct, rebuke and encourage—with great patience and careful instruction (2 Timothy 4:2).*

### SHARING YOUR LIFE AND FAITH

With whom should we share the Gospel? The answer is simple—with everyone! We should consider every person we meet a divine appointment. We should be constantly "tuned in" to people, considering how to turn a conversation to spiritual matters and an opportunity to share the Gospel. Two principles can help direct your energy more productively.

### *Start at the center of your "circle"*

When Jesus told His disciples to share the Gospel, He told them to start with their innermost circle.

*"But you will receive power when the Holy Spirit comes on you; and you will be my witnesses in Jerusalem, and in all Judea and Samaria, and to the ends of the earth" (Acts 1:8).*

Jerusalem is where they were located, and Judea was the region surrounding their city. Samaria was the next neighboring country. The "ends of the earth" encompassed every possible place. Jesus told them to begin at the center of their smallest circle, then work out from there.

You, too, have concentric circles of friends and acquaintances. Your inner circle contains people you know the best. Outer circles are composed of more distant friends and relatives.

The inner circle is the most natural place to start. You know more people in that circle by name and by needs, people with whom you've formed friendships and working partnerships. These people have the opportunity to closely observe your life. Within the inner circle you can expect to have the most opportunities to share the Gospel with people who will really listen.

Who are the people in your inner circle? If you are aboard a ship, it includes your bunkmates and all those who closely surround you. In an Army unit, it's those in your platoon. In an Air

Force unit, it might be members of your element, flight, or shop. In all branches of service, it includes roommates or close neighbors. If you participate in a club, team, or voluntary organization, it includes those people as well. In short, your inner circle consists of people you know the best and who know you best. Begin sharing the Gospel with these people, then work out to the larger circles.

### Let the sick know about the "physician"

> On hearing this, Jesus said to them, "It is not the healthy who need a doctor, but the sick. I have not come to call the righteous, but sinners" (Mark 2:17).

We know that all have sinned and fallen short of God's plan (Romans 3:23, Isaiah 53:6), but some are more aware of their spiritual sickness than others. People who know they need a physician are more likely to take notes when someone gives directions to the closest doctor's office.

Christians sometimes distance themselves from people involved in obvious sin, yet Jesus seemed particularly friendly with these people. In His day, many "great sinners" were the first to come to Him for salvation. Those who are suffering the self-inflicted wounds of their own foolishness are often more willing to hear a message about forgiveness and healing.

> "And if you spend yourselves in behalf of the hungry and satisfy the needs of the oppressed, then your light will rise in the darkness, and your night will become like the noonday. The LORD will guide you always; he will satisfy your needs in a sun-scorched land and will strengthen your frame. You will be like a well-watered garden, like a spring whose waters never fail" (Isaiah 58:10–11, emphasis added).

A list of multiple blessings follows this command to spend ourselves for the hungry and the oppressed. If we do this, God promises to bless us.

As we grow and mature in our walk with Christ, we become better listeners. We hear not just the words people say, but what they really mean. From their eyes and their demeanor we can see their emotional and spiritual condition. In every soul there is a hunger to know God and to be assured of forgiveness of sin and eternal life. Learn to become attentive to people's needs.

## EVANGELISM CLOSE UP

Ray and Jake were soldiers assigned to temporary duty at a military leadership school. Both had served several years in the military. Both were married and had small children. Ray was a Christian; Jake was an avowed atheist. As the two men carpooled to their class, they discussed the class, their families and children, and their views on many other subjects. Occasionally they talked about God. Ray shared his faith in Jesus and his views on God, while Jake explained why he did not believe in God. And so it went every day, 20 minutes to school and 20 minutes back, sharing, listening, discussing.

As the weeks passed, Jake became interested in what the Bible had to say about marriage and raising children. He had already been divorced once and wanted his second marriage to last. He was also struggling to discipline his two-year-old and was looking for good advice wherever he could find it. Jake was pleasantly surprised when Ray showed him the Bible's wise guidance on marriage and parenting. Eventually, Jake accepted an invitation to attend church with Ray. There he heard more about the God of the Bible, new life in Christ, and assurance of eternal life. A few months later, Jake prayed to receive Jesus as his personal Savior and Lord. Ray and Jake both rejoiced that God had brought them together for a short time and worked out the circumstances for them to carpool. In a short time, Jake was transformed from a convinced atheist to a converted Christian. Ray's daily sharing of his life, his faith, and appropriate verses helped Jake with his most important issues, eventually leading him to faith in God.

Ray's testimony came through his actions and his words. He also prayed regularly for his friend. The Spirit of God softened Jake's hard heart and helped him understand the grace of God. Although Ray did not feel he was much of an evangelist, God used his faithful sharing of life and words to lead Jake to Christ. Every soldier, sailor, and airman can do the same with a few friends and coworkers in their inner circle. God will bring the results.

Our job as Christ's ambassadors in the military is to show the hungry where there is "bread" and help the hurting find relief.

> . . . *that God was reconciling the world to himself in Christ, not counting men's sins against them. And he has committed to us the message of reconciliation. We are therefore* Christ's ambassadors, *as though God were making his appeal through us. We implore you on Christ's behalf: Be reconciled to God (2 Corinthians 5:19–20, emphasis added).*

 **SUMMARY**

- ✤ Christians inside the military community are best situated to share the Gospel with their peers.
- ✤ The Gospel is best communicated with words matched by actions.
- ✤ Be prepared to give a brief explanation of how you became a Christian and how it changed you.
- ✤ Be able to give a brief explanation of the Gospel and to encourage others to express faith in Jesus.

# Making Disciples

*Then Jesus came to them and said, "All authority in heaven and on earth has been given to me. Therefore* go and make disciples *of all nations, baptizing them in the name of the Father and of the Son and of the Holy Spirit, and teaching them to obey everything I have commanded you. And surely I am with you always, to the very end of the age" (Matthew 28:18–20, emphasis added).*

EVERY CHRISTIAN HAS THE OPPORTUNITY to invest in others, helping them grow in Christ and become disciples. The Great Commission Jesus gave His followers was to "go and make *disciples.*" His disciples were to preach the Gospel, starting in Jerusalem, then Judea and all of Samaria, and then to the uttermost parts of the world. But preaching the Gospel was only the first step of the Great Commission. The ultimate goal was not just to win new believers, but to develop mature disciples.

## FROM INFANCY TO MATURITY

To understand the difference between new Christians and disciples, consider the example of a newborn baby. A new believer is like a baby, alive and equipped for growth but unable to function alone. A new believer grows into a disciple when he has matured and is able to spiritually feed, protect, and provide for himself. Additionally, disciples are able to reproduce after their own kind, that is, to make new disciples. Ideally, every new believer should grow up to be an *adult* believer, but this doesn't always happen. The author of Hebrews chided his readers for their continued immaturity:

> *In fact, though by this time you ought to be teachers, you need someone to teach you the elementary truths of God's word all over again. You need milk, not solid food! Anyone who lives on milk, being still an infant, is not acquainted with the teaching about righteousness. But solid food is for the mature, who by constant use have trained themselves to distinguish good from evil. Therefore let us leave the elementary teachings about Christ and* go on to maturity *(Hebrews 5:12–6:1b, emphasis added).*

The pattern God established for spiritual growth is exactly like the one in our physical bodies. We are born, we grow up, and we learn from our parents and teachers. As we mature, we take our place as productive members of society. We reproduce life when we have children. Most of this we do without much thought; the process just happens. Our bodies mature and develop without much work on our part. If we eat, exercise, and sleep, we grow.

The stages of spiritual life should parallel our physical lives. We are born when we receive Jesus as Lord and Savior. We grow as we feed on the Word of God and learn from spiritual "parents" and teachers. We mature when we reproduce ourselves spiritually by making new disciples. The difference between physical and spiritual maturity is this: Spiritual growth requires our concentrated effort.

Baby believers can and will remain that way unless they feed on God's Word and exercise faith in fellowship with other believers. Like infants, spiritual babes are susceptible to disease and vulnerable to attack. It is the responsibility of mature believers to care for and teach "baby" Christians. Today, this responsibility often goes ignored. After new Christians are born into the Kingdom, few are properly followed up and nurtured.

The initial responsibility for discipleship training lies with the person(s) who introduces a new believer to Christ. Just as we would not expect a new baby to fend for himself, to find food and clothing, we should not assume a new Christian automatically seeks spiritual nourishment and knows how to get it. Discipling should start within a week, if not an hour, of the moment a person receives Christ. We do not need to make the new believer "hungry." The Spirit of God does that. Rather, we need to introduce hungry new Christians to the milk of God's Word and help them make it part of their daily lives.

*Like newborn babies, crave pure spiritual milk, so that by it you may grow up in your salvation (1 Peter 2:2).*

## MAKING DISCIPLES: THE COMMAND AND THE PLAN

The Great Commission in Matthew 28 requires Jesus' disciples to make other disciples. Instructions for how to do this are given in 2 Timothy 2:2:

*And the things you have heard me say in the presence of many witnesses entrust to reliable men who will also be qualified to teach others.*

This is a profoundly simple plan. The goal is for qualified men and women to teach others. That part sounds a lot like the verse in Matthew. Where will these qualified men and women disciples come from? They will be raised up and taught by other reliable men and women. Paul chose Timothy to select others and teach them the things he had learned from Paul.

Paul picked Timothy because he was a reliable man. He taught Timothy: 1) how to be a mature disciple and 2) how to pass on what he had learned to others. Maturing Christians become disciples and, in the process, begin to comprehend their responsibility to help others grow up in Christ. The disciple becomes a discipler.

If this is the first time you've considered 2 Timothy 2:2, you may be surprised. Is every Christian "authorized" and encouraged to participate in disciplemaking? Yes! Perhaps you thought when you became a Christian you were just going to hang out, living a righteous life until Jesus returned. That's important, but Jesus has much more intended for His disciples. He has given us the responsibility and privilege of sharing the Gospel and helping to disciple new believers.

Let's make Paul's mandate more personal by inserting your own name: "[YOUR NAME], the things you learned from your spiritual teachers as you were growing up in Christ, teach and model those things to others. [YOUR NAME], select faithful, reliable *others,* who will in turn be able to carry on the training with others, who will teach others, and still others."

You get the idea? Discipleship training is to be conducted by disciples; its goal is to produce disciples from baby Christians; the new disciples are to continue the cycle.

The best disciplemaker in the military environment is you, another military person. Disciplemaking is not dependent on a schedule of chapel services or structured events. It does not have to fall through the cracks during deployment or aboard ships. A more mature believer can mentor a new Christian anywhere in the world, under any conditions. If you are committed to building up mature followers of Christ, discipleship can continue, uninterrupted, even in the ever-changing climate of the military. It can be done on the go as you move through all of life's experiences. The word "go" ("Go and make disciples") in Matthew 28:18 is more accurately translated, *"having gone on your way"* or *"as you are going on your way."* This is a present-tense verb implying continuous action.

Maybe you've read Matthew 28:18–20 and thought, "Someday I will *go* someplace—Africa or some other faraway place—and make disciples." That is not what this verse means. Jesus instructed His disciples to go on with their lives, and while they were going, to make disciples! It is not a command to move someplace; it's not limited to a certain period of time. It is a command that implies life-on-life training while Christians go about their lives.

A word of caution here: Personal disciplemaking should not take the place of the church. Disciples need fellowship and need to be around people with different gifts. Discipleship training also does not replace seminary, Bible college courses, or other formal instruction. Again, think of the example of a baby. A baby is fed and trained by her parents to eat, exercise, think, and be responsible. She will learn skills and habits from her parents that are essential to a healthy life. Then she will grow up and learn to develop her particular strengths into an occupation. This additional training is often learned on the job or in college. The training that the baby, the child, the youth, the adolescent received from the parent is not replaced by the occupational training; rather, occupational training builds on early life-skills training. The same is true of discipleship, which equips new Christians with the basics and prepares them for more advanced spiritual training later.

All Christians need to grow and mature. They need to survive the early temptation to go back to their old ways. They need to develop edifying relationships with Christian peers. They need to learn how to "eat" and to "digest" God's Word. They need to learn how to pray and experience God at work. They need to learn how to communicate their beliefs in a simple and understandable way to others. The apostle Paul summarized this fundamental training this way:

*So, naturally, we proclaim Christ! We warn everyone we meet, and we teach everyone we can, all that we know about him, so that we may bring every man up to his full maturity in Christ. This is what I am working and struggling at, with all the strength that God puts into me. (Colossians 1:28–29, PHILLIPS).*

God didn't entrust this work only to Paul, or to the clergy, or to missionaries. It's what God asks of anyone who wishes to do what Jesus did. And there's certainly no shortage of work to be done. Jesus told the first 12 disciples:

*"The harvest is plentiful but the workers are few. Ask the Lord of the harvest, therefore, to send out workers into his harvest field" (Matthew 9:37–38).*

Becoming a mature disciple and discipling another person are choices. Too few have chosen to grow to their full maturity in Christ. Fewer still have chosen to pass on what they have learned to younger Christians. If we choose to do these things, God will bless our obedience. He will bless our lives in many ways as we pour ourselves into others. Consider this promise:

*"If you spend yourselves in behalf of the hungry and satisfy the needs of the oppressed, then your light will rise in the darkness, and your night will become like the noonday. The LORD will guide you always; he will satisfy your needs in a sun-scorched land and will strengthen your frame. You will be like a well-watered garden, like a spring whose waters never fail" (Isaiah 58:10–11).*

## THE SPECIFICS OF DISCIPLEMAKING

"OK," you say, "I'm convinced. I want to make disciples. But how do I do it? How many people can I disciple at one time? How long will it take?"

Several outstanding books detail the specifics of disciple-making. Among them are *The Lost Art of Disciple Making* (Zondervan) by LeRoy Eims and *Personal Disciple Making* (Here's Life Publishers, P.O. Box 1576, San Bernadino, CA 92402) by Christopher B. Adsit. Of course, the best book on disciplemaking is already at your fingertips. It's the Bible. Jesus made disciples. Paul made disciples. Peter made disciples. Their experiences are recorded in the Bible for you to study and emulate.

### *How long?*

Spiritual growth varies with each individual. The amount of time you have available to spend will affect your progress. The disciple's hunger and desire to change make a big difference as well. Your experience as a trainer is another factor. Jesus spent three years on earth with His disciples. By the third year, He sent them out to minister and teach. Becoming a disciple is a lifelong journey, but it is not unreasonable for a new Christian to develop fundamental disciplines and knowledge in a two-year period. This time frame works well in the military. Most assignments last three or four years. This gives a disciplemaker about the right time to spend with a new Christian before they part ways.

Although geography may separate you, you can continue to disciple someone by phone, e-mail, and regular mail. Often, the relationship between the disciple and his first spiritual mentor is unique. The disciple may have other teachers, but only one "first" discipler. Make every effort to maintain the early disci-pling relationship using the technologies available today. Do all you can to ensure that the new believer becomes well established in his faith and connected with other believers at the next duty station.

### How many?

Jesus picked 12 to be with Him. Paul had from two to eight that traveled with him, but both he and Jesus were in full-time ministry. As a military person, you have a job, perhaps a family, and many other responsibilities. Because you have less discretionary time, start with one disciple and learn your capacity. Anyone can find time to disciple one other person. Two or three is probably the upper limit for someone with a full-time job and other responsibilities.

### How?

Although this book is not a "how-to" guide on disciplemaking, we should look at the method Jesus and Paul used to make disciples. Both Jesus and Paul *modeled* the behavior and actions they taught. They used *their own lives* as their primary teaching tool. We have become accustomed to teachers who tell us what to believe or what to do, but do not necessarily follow their own teaching. This was not true of Jesus and Paul. They basically said, "Watch what I am doing, and do the same thing."

> Jesus' words: *"A new command I give you: Love one another. As I have loved you, so you must love one another" (John 13:34).*

> Paul's words: *You became imitators of us and of the Lord; in spite of severe suffering, you welcomed the message with the joy given by the Holy Spirit. And so you became a model to all the believers in Macedonia and Achaia (1 Thessalonians 1:6–7).*

The 12 disciples learned to live like Jesus by doing what He did. The Thessalonian church learned to live like Christians by imitating Paul. By doing this, they became a model for other believers. We learn best what we see lived out in others. By the time Paul had finished discipling Timothy, he was able to say:

*You, however, know all about my teaching, my way of life, my purpose, faith, patience, love, endurance, persecutions, sufferings—what kinds of things happened to me in Antioch, Iconium and Lystra, the persecutions I endured (2 Timothy 3:10–11a).*

By observing Paul in different circumstances, Timothy learned how to live an obedient and disciplined life. He imitated what he saw in Paul. In doing so, he became more like Paul, who had himself become like Jesus.

This pattern for making disciples is clearly demonstrated in the lives of Jesus and the early disciples:

(Jesus) *"I have set you an example that you should do as I have done for you" (John 13:15).*

(Paul) *Don't let anyone look down on you because you are young, but set an example for the believers in speech, in life, in love, in faith and in purity (1 Timothy 4:12).*

(Paul) *In everything set them an example by doing what is good. In your teaching show integrity, seriousness . . . (Titus 2:7).*

(Peter) *To this you were called, because Christ suffered for you, leaving you an example, that you should follow in his steps (1 Peter 2:21).*

This pattern is repeated often in the New Testament. It is, undeniably, the way established by Jesus and the early church for teaching disciples, yet it is remarkably rare in the modern church. It is nonetheless a timeless principle. If we are going to fulfill the whole teaching of the Great Commission, we need to make disciples. To make disciples, we need to walk in a way that will instruct others. We can take a disciple no further than we have gone. We cannot teach what we do not experience in our own walk with Christ. No one will naturally do what the teacher does not do, even if the teacher talks about it every day. Our lives validate what we teach. This is the single most important tool in making disciples.

Consider these verses, testimony of Paul's training of the disciples in Thessalonica:

*But we were gentle among you, like a mother caring for her little children. We loved you so much that we were delighted to share with you* not only the gospel of God but our lives as well, *because you had become so dear to us (1 Thessalonians 2:7–8, emphasis added).*

*You are witnesses, and so is God, of how holy, righteous and blameless we were among you who believed. For you know that we dealt with each of you as a father deals with his own children (1 Thessalonians 2:10–11).*

Maybe this life-on-life method of disciplemaking is making you feel a little uneasy. You may be thinking, "I'm not sure my life and my activities are a good pattern for another Christian." It's true, there is no greater motivation to walk in a way that is true to the Gospel than when another person is watching and patterning their life after you. If you're going to be a disciplemaker, you have the responsibility to walk in obedience to

Christ so your life can be a model for others.

## A SPECIAL RELATIONSHIP

A discipling relationship goes much deeper than teacher and trainer. A discipler not only teaches but shares from his own life and experiences. A discipler cares for his friend like a mother and encourages him like a father. Out of this relationship grows a healthy, fruitful disciple who is able to do the same thing for the next spiritual generation.

 **SUMMARY**

- ✦ The military culture provides a framework for disciplemaking.
- ✦ The closeness of life in military quarters and work environments allows others to closely observe your life.
- ✦ It's easier to disciple someone when you share similar circumstances.
- ✦ Every Christian is responsible to help other believers grow up to be mature, fruitful Christians.
- ✦ The tools of discipling are the Bible and prayer.
- ✦ Most of what a new believer retains will be what you demonstrate in your own life.

# Chaplains, Chapels, Churches, and Organizations

*When you go to war against your enemies and see horses and chariots and an army greater than yours, do not be afraid of them, because the Lord your God, who brought you up out of Egypt, will be with you. When you are about to go into battle, the priest shall come forward and address the army (Deuteronomy 20:1–2, emphasis added).*

THE MILITARY IS AN ORGANIZATION like no other. Its people are nomadic, moving from assignment to assignment. Their work often takes them away from their homes and families. Because of their unique, highly mobile lifestyle, soldiers, sailors, and airmen need spiritual leadership from a pastor who understands and shares the hardships of military life.

For this reason, the military chaplain service was established. Although clergymen served alongside soldiers as far back as the 1600s, General George Washington formalized the chaplaincy in 1775. Since that time, chaplains' responsibilities have changed and grown in response to the needs of the military. From Valley Forge to Yorktown, Bull Run to Appomattox, Guadalcanal to Iwo Jima, Saigon to Seoul, military chaplains have served side-by-side with American warriors. Chaplains have ministered in trenches and hospitals, aboard ships and airplanes. They have conducted funeral and memorial services for countless warriors who paid the ultimate price. Chaplains serve as advisers on staffs of generals and commanders. They provide a visible reminder of the importance of following God and guide ethical behavior by example and teaching. It would be impossible to tell the history of the U.S. military without including the contributions of its chaplains, yet their heroic and honorable service has generally gone unheralded.

### WHAT IS A CHAPLAIN?

Chaplains are ministers who serve on active duty in all branches of the military. Representatives of their denominations and commissioned officers, they are "citizen-soldiers" like the people they minister to. Instead of carrying the weapons that most soldiers use, they are armed with the "sword of the Spirit," the Word of God. Equipped with hearts of service and mercy, they are leaders in worship and counselors to the community. They model earthly citizenship and heavenly allegiance. Chaplains are ambassadors of their church and the Kingdom of God. A commander has many people on his staff—experts in communications, civil engineering, personnel, and strategy. Chaplains are on equal level with these advisers. They are called on to pray for wisdom and guidance. General George Patton once asked his chaplain to pray for clear weather!

Chaplains serve men and women at bases, posts, and ports and travel with soldiers to faraway battle zones. Their ministry takes them into duty sections, offices, and dormitories. Few people have the access to military people that chaplains do. Their work is demanding, their hours long and rigorous. The benefit chaplains provide to their people is immeasurable.

## A CHAPLAIN'S WORK

Military people are entitled to exercise their First Amendment right to worship while assigned anywhere in the world. Chaplains make this possible. They provide the place and the resources for military members to participate in group worship of God. Some chaplains have an office in a building, but in the highly mobile 21st century, chaplains can be found on a hangar deck, in a tent, or on any plot of ground under the sky. The place is not as important as providing the opportunity to worship.

Christian chaplains minister to diverse faith groups and rarely share the same denominational background as the majority of their congregation. Other chaplains come from Jewish and Muslim faiths. Regardless of their background or affiliation, all chaplains provide these basic services:

➤ Leading worship
➤ Advising military leaders
➤ Conducting weddings
➤ Performing baptisms
➤ Leading funerals and memorial services
➤ Teaching spiritual truth
➤ Counseling individuals
➤ Mentoring lay leaders

Chaplains are the exclusive providers of these services in the military. They also participate in the "housekeeping" tasks required of all military people: developing long- and short-range plans, budgeting, handling personnel matters, and maintaining their uniforms, personal appearance, and duty space within military standards. They participate in military exercises, prepare for deployments, and ship out to every corner of the world where military people serve.

*It was he who gave some to be apostles, some to be*

*prophets, some to be evangelists, and some to be pastors
and teachers, to prepare God's people for works of service, so that the body of Christ may be built up until we all
reach unity in the faith and in the knowledge of the Son of
God and become mature, attaining to the whole measure
of the fullness of Christ (Ephesians 4:11–13).*

Chaplains are gifted pastors called to military ministry. Military chaplains are unique from other kinds of pastors, with
advantages and disadvantages compared to pastors in local
churches. The mobility of military life accounts for most of the
differences. Pastors in local churches often know everyone in
the congregation. They may stay in one place long enough to
know families for two or three generations. This is not true in
the military, where the entire population at a base changes every
three years. A typical pastor counsels only members of his or her
own congregation. A chaplain counsels all kinds of military people sent to him by referral, but few of these people attend chap-
lain-led worship services.

Chaplains may be deployed at a moment's notice to a distant location with a group of warriors they've never met. They
are expected to meet people and provide spiritual guidance,
service, and leadership to these relative strangers. Then, as
quickly as they arrive, they return to their home base, post, or
ship at the deployment's conclusion.

## WHAT IS A CHAPEL?

One of a chaplain's key responsibilities is to organize chapel
services. But what is chapel? Is it a church? In the larger sense of
*"the Church,"* which is the body of Christ, the chapel is certainly
a church. It is composed of many believers, each uniquely gifted,
each contributing to the spiritual well-being of one another.

*Now to each one the manifestation of the Spirit is given
for the common good. . . . Now you are the body of Christ,
and each one of you is a part of it (1 Corinthians 12:7, 27).*

Christians were not meant to thrive on their own. Everyone
needs fellowship with other believers, in the same way one
ember needs other hot coals to continue burning brightly. In
many locations, the chapel is the only place to find this kind of
fellowship. This is especially true in remote locations, in foreign
assignments where English is not the primary language, on
ships at sea, and even on some remote U.S. bases. For many military Christians, the chapel is the only body of believers available. It's possible to spend an entire career in the military and
never attend a civilian community church.

In most chapels, you can expect to grow as a Christian, use
your gifts, and be built up by the spiritual gifts of others. Most
chapels offer a choir, develop Sunday school programs for families, and sponsor age- and interest-specific small groups.
Chapels are *nearly* full-service congregations. However, they are
not churches, and for good reason.

The U.S. Constitution does not allow the government to
establish a church. It encourages citizens to exercise their own
judgment in choosing a religion and practicing it according to
their beliefs. For the military to establish a church, it would
violate the Constitution, which every military person swears to
uphold. Yet the government realizes that an active-duty soldier
cannot count on the presence of a local church at every assignment, especially in the combat zones where they are most
likely to need it. For this reason, a balance is struck. While not
establishing a church, the government provides for the free
exercise of religion. This balance is an important one. The
right to provide chapels and chaplains has been challenged in
court several times. Each time, the court has upheld the right

of service men and women to practice their religion and the right of the government to provide chaplains. This issue will continue to be challenged, so it's important for everyone in the military to understand their constitutional right to chapels and chaplains.

## WHAT A CHAPEL IS NOT

A chapel is not a local church, not a denomination, not an instrument of the government. So how do these limitations affect the organization and operation of a chapel?

First, a chapel will almost always be manned by chaplains from several denominations. Most chapels conduct different types of worship services, such as liturgical and contemporary. Most chapels provide worship services and educational programs for Protestants and Roman Catholics. Some will also have services for Greek and Russian Orthodox Christians.

Second, there is no "membership" in a chapel. Remember, a base or post turns over its entire population in a matter of a few years. Some remote locations experience 100-percent turnover every year. Romans 12:5 reminds us, "In Christ we who are many form one body, and each *member* belongs to all the others" (emphasis added). While military people will never be members of a chapel, they are still members with other believers in the Church, which is Christ's body of believers.

Third, chaplains are not required to perform a function that would violate their conscience or denominational beliefs. For example, a chaplain who believes baptism is only for those who have expressed saving faith in Jesus is not required to baptize an infant. But that chaplain will help the parents find either a pastor or another chaplain to perform the baptism.

Chaplains are not permitted to preach denominational doctrine as the "only way" to believe. Does this lead to a watered-down Gospel? Not at all. Christian chaplains "major on the majors" of practical Christian living. They focus on common ground rather than on peripheral doctrinal differences. This environment tends to strengthen an individual's belief rather than weaken it. Each believer is encouraged—even challenged—to search the Bible to determine what it says on issues of faith in practice. Because of this, believers are often stretched and shaped in ways not possible in other environments. Chaplains focus their preaching, teaching, and counseling on the specific needs of military people. Few of the core issues of life are impacted by the doctrinal variations of denominations.

## CHAPEL ORGANIZATIONS

If you're new to the military, you may be overwhelmed with all of its acronyms—OIC, CINCPAC, ETIC, and hundreds of others. The chapel also has its own lexicon, including PMOC, PWOC, PYOC, and JOY. Each of these is a chapel organization, although the names vary among the branches of service. The functions, however, are similar throughout. These organizations are set up by chaplains as a way to provide fellowship for people with similar interests. Some of the major groups include:

➤ Chapel council (planning and organizing)
➤ Funds advisory council (administration)
➤ Men of the chapel (fellowship and challenge to grow in Christ)
➤ Christian education team (Sunday school teachers)
➤ Women of the chapel (fellowship and challenge)
➤ Youth (social events and peer support)
➤ Singles (encouragement and challenge)
➤ Single parents (support and assistance)
➤ Choir (worship and praise)
➤ Bible study groups (growth and fellowship)
➤ Dessert/dinner groups (fellowship)

These groups are organized by the chapel staff but are rarely run by the chaplains. A chaplain serves as an adviser, while laypeople use their gifts to provide the bulk of the leadership.

Chaplains, like church pastors, cannot do all of the work. Individual believers are encouraged to use their gifts to fill in the gaps and contribute to the congregation. God equipped some to be apostles, some to be prophets, some to be evangelists, and some to be pastors and teachers to prepare God's people for works of service (Ephesians 4:11–12). These gifts are given to spiritual leaders to build up other believers, who in turn carry on works of service. Chapel organizations provide the platform for individual Christians to serve and accomplish the work of God. The full potential of a Christian fellowship, whether a local church or chapel, is maximized when every believer uses his or her unique gifting in a congregation of mutually committed followers of Jesus.

> *Just as each of us has one body with many members, and these members do not all have the same function, so in Christ we who are many form one body, and each member belongs to all the others. We have different gifts, according to the grace given us. If a man's gift is prophesying, let him use it in proportion to his faith. If it is serving, let him serve; if it is teaching, let him teach; if it is encouraging, let him encourage; if it is contributing to the needs of others, let him give generously; if it is leadership, let him govern diligently; if it is showing mercy, let him do it cheerfully (Romans 12:4–8).*

## WHERE TO WORSHIP

Should you worship, fellowship, and contribute to the body of believers at the chapel, or should you fulfill your spiritual purposes in the context of a local church? This is a question every military Christian faces. The answer will be different depending on your assignments, life issues, and local circumstances. Here are some factors to consider at each new assignment:

➤ Where can you maximize your service to Christ?

➤ How far away is your place of worship?

➤ Which place best meets your family's needs and allows the most opportunities to serve?

➤ If you deploy, leaving your family behind, which option will best meet your family's needs while you're gone?

➤ Where do your friends, neighbors, and coworkers worship?

➤ Where would you feel most comfortable taking a non-Christian or a new Christian?

➤ Where are the conditions best to stimulate your growth and encourage your daily obedience to God?

That's a lot to think about. If possible, make this decision slowly, prayerfully, and only once during each assignment. It takes time to build trust and relationships. Changing fellowship groups in the middle of an assignment can produce months of spiritual stagnation and frustration.

Sometimes the choice will be easy. In a few places, you won't have many options. Most overseas chapels have relatively large, diverse congregations because of the limited number of English-speaking churches available. Incidentally, these large, mixed congregations are often the most dynamic, resulting in significant growth and service opportunities.

## OTHER ORGANIZATIONS

The 20th century saw the rise of hundreds of parachurch organizations, groups outside of the church that tend to be strong in a specific aspect of ministry, such as evangelism or Bible study. Some parachurch organizations have developed expertise in ministry to military people. At almost any military installation at home or abroad, you can expect to find The Navigators,

113

Campus Crusade for Christ, Cadence International, Officer's Christian Fellowship, Bible Club Movement, and others. These organizations have trained staff and resources to minister to the unique needs and challenges of military people. Men and women serving overseas may also benefit from local missionaries, who occasionally enlist support from Americans GIs.

The emphasis of most military parachurch organizations is training soldiers to minister within their own units. These uniquely gifted missionaries help chaplains equip people for personal victory and fruitful ministry. Thousands of service members have received significant help in their relationship with God through these organizations.

## CONFLICT OR COOPERATION?

Do parachurch groups help or hurt the ministry of the chapel? Do they drain resources or provide additional resources? The body of Christ cannot have internal competition and conflict; each ministering part must be coordinated with the others. Each group should concentrate its efforts on what it does best (disciplemaking, evangelism, hospitality, etc.) while seeking to equip growing disciples for ministry.

> But in fact God has arranged the parts in the body, every one of them, just as he wanted them to be. If they were all one part, where would the body be? As it is, there are many parts, but one body. The eye cannot say to the hand, "I don't need you!" And the head cannot say to the feet, "I don't need you!" (1 Corinthians 12:18–21).

The "authorized" spiritual outlet at a base, post, ship, or port is the chapel. Chaplains are responsible for the ministry at their location. When the inspector general (IG) evaluates ministry quality and opportunity at any location, it is the chaplain who must answer for the activity, service, and success of the spiritual programs. Churches and parachurches should coordinate their work with military chaplains.

## FIND AND USE YOUR SPIRITUAL RESOURCES

Worship and fellowship are important for all believers, especially those in the military. Military people often face remote and dangerous duty locations. Even while stationed near large cities, military people find that their interests and needs do not always mesh with local churches. In response, chaplains and chapel services have been established to meet the unique and changing needs of military people.

Seek out fellowship that best meets your needs and an environment in which you can contribute to the spiritual welfare of others, whether that is in a chapel or a local church. Don't attempt to be a Christian loner. Find your chaplain, learn what the chapel can do for you, and find an outlet to minister to others.

 **SUMMARY**

- ✦ All Christians need to be "plugged in" to a local fellowship to survive and be fruitful.
- ✦ The U.S. Constitution provides for its soldiers to exercise their right to worship.
- ✦ This provision has been embodied in military chaplains.
- ✦ A chapel is not a local church, but it does minister to people who are part of the body of Christ.
- ✦ Chaplains provide unique ministry, tailored to the needs of military service members.
- ✦ A fruitful chapel congregation coordinates the abilities of its people and maximizes their gifts and calling.
- ✦ Parachurch organizations are a valuable supplement to the chapel, equipping military people to minister to their comrades.

# Servanthood in the Service

*Jesus called them together and said, "You know that the rulers of the Gentiles lord it over them, and their high officials exercise authority over them. Not so with you. Instead,* whoever wants to become great among you must be your servant, *and whoever wants to be first must be your slave—just as the Son of Man did not come to be served, but to serve, and to give his life as a ransom for many" (Matthew 20:25–28, emphasis added).*

JESUS TOLD HIS DISCIPLES that the power-wielding, abusive leadership they were used to was not part of God's plan. In His plan for godly leadership, those who served would become the great ones. To make the point clearer, Jesus demonstrated this kind of leadership by His own example.

As we carefully consider His command and His example, it's easy to see the merit in the method. A leader who extracts performance by force and positional power achieves, at best, exactly what he asks for and no more. A leader who guides with wisdom, while looking out for the needs of his people, will be surprised at the levels of performance subordinates achieve. A selfless leader earns trust from followers.

Major General John M. Scholfield, in his graduation address to the West Point class of 1879, said it this way:

"The discipline which makes the soldiers of a free country reliable in battle is not to be gained by harsh or tyrannical treatment. On the contrary, such treatment is far more likely to destroy than to make an army. It is possible to impart instruction and give commands in such a manner and such a tone of voice as to inspire in the soldier no feeling but an intense desire to obey, while the opposite manner and tone of voice cannot fail to incite strong resentment and a desire to disobey. The one mode or the other of dealing with subordinates springs from a corresponding spirit in the breast of the commander. He who feels the respect which is due to others cannot fail to inspire in them respect for himself, while he who feels, and hence manifests disrespect towards others, especially his subordinates, cannot fail to inspire hatred against himself" (from the Air Force Academy Cadet Handbook).

## A MODEL OF SERVANT LEADERSHIP

Is it possible to adopt and live out Jesus' value system in today's military? Does the same standard apply to senior NCOs and officers, as well as junior officers and lower-ranking enlisted men and women? Yes! It's not only possible, it is required of all who follow Jesus.

Jesus understood power. He was, after all, the Son of God. Yet He demonstrated personal restraint in order to achieve greater ends. Consider His restraint at the moment of His arrest in the Garden of Gethsemane. Surrounded by armed soldiers, outnumbered and facing desperate circumstances, Jesus told His disciples:

> "Do you think I cannot call on my Father, and he will at once put at my disposal more than twelve legions of angels?" (Matthew 26:53).

Now that is real power! Yet Jesus demonstrated amazing self-control. At His disposal He had all the power He needed to save Himself, yet He chose instead to obey His Father and save humanity for all time.

Throughout His earthly ministry, Jesus demonstrated this servant leadership. No one doubted that Jesus was the leader of His followers. The disciples, the Jewish leaders, Jesus' own family, and the multitudes He spoke to all understood that Jesus was the leader. But they were surprised that He did not act like other people in authority. His disciples were shocked when Jesus washed their feet, a servant's task. Jesus challenged their thinking when He explained His actions:

> *"Do you understand what I have done for you?" he asked them. "You call me 'Teacher' and 'Lord,' and rightly so, for that is what I am. Now that I, your Lord and Teacher, have washed your feet, you also should wash one another's feet. I have set you an example that you should do as I have done for you. I tell you the truth, no servant is greater than his master, nor is a messenger greater than the one who sent him. Now that you know these things, you will be blessed if you do them" (John 13:12b–17, emphasis added).*

By His own actions, Jesus demonstrated what was required of servant leaders. His actions were clear, and He told the disciples to do the same thing. He also promised that they would be blessed if they obeyed.

### SERVANTHOOD REDEFINED

Servants and leaders may seem at opposite ends of the power spectrum. In most societies, servants come from the lower classes. But if we think of being a servant as an occupation or a level in society, we miss Jesus' point. He redefined service and servanthood. The world says, "Acts of service are performed by servants." Jesus, making a subtle but important distinction, said, "Those who perform acts of service are servants." The characterization of a person as a servant flows from actions, not position. Title follows function, not the other way around.

Is this a small point? Is it merely semantics? Not at all. Historically, democratic countries have called their government officials "public servants." This meant individuals left the pursuit of personal goals and adopted a philosophy and lifestyle of service to their community or nation. Although some modern politicians have demeaned the high view of public service by their own selfish behavior, the idea of "public service" is still a valid one.

## SERVICE IN THE MILITARY

Serving in the military is one type of public service. In fact, the word "serve" is used frequently to describe someone's work in the military. Corporately, the branches of the military (Army, Navy, Air Force, Marines, and Coast Guard) are referred to as *the service*. A high school student might say, "I'm going to join *the service* when I graduate." Selected college students attend the *service academies*. Military recruiting slogans make ample use of the word "serve." "Proudly we *serve!*" declares the U.S. Marine Corps. The Code of Conduct for members of the Armed Forces of the United States begins with this statement: "I am an American, fighting in the forces which guard my country and our way of life. I am prepared to give my life in their defense." The concepts of serving and being prepared to lay down one's life are fundamental to the military.

Christians in the military are in service to Jesus as well as to their country. It is entirely compatible for Christians to be servants, soldiers, and leaders. If we see service as something we *willingly do,* rather than a level in society or an occupation, the inconsistencies evaporate and the possibilities emerge.

How, then, can you fulfill your obligations to the government and to the commands of Jesus in the area of servanthood? How can you, at any rank, consistently fulfill the twofold responsibility to serve God and man? You can do this by meeting the needs of others, using the resources and authority entrusted to you by God and the military. Here is a definition worth remembering:

**A servant is one who sees a need and meets it, without being asked and without expecting reward.**

How simple, how profound, how applicable to every situation! Service starts and ends in the heart, the innermost person. To consistently serve, determine in your heart to look for opportunities to meet the needs of others. Remind yourself that an act of service is the reward, and look for no other. Your best intentions to serve will not succeed without a deep, internal commitment. It must be one of the fundamental values that guides all of your actions. In the Bible, Paul stated the challenge this way:

> *Do nothing out of selfish ambition or vain conceit, but in humility consider others better than yourselves. Each of you should look not only to your own interests, but also to the interests of others (Philippians 2:3–4).*

Jesus had this to say about a servant attitude:

> *"So you also, when you have done everything you were told to do, should say, 'We are unworthy servants; we have only done our duty'" (Luke 17:10).*

We're reminded in the Old Testament that servanthood flows from the heart, but the eye initiates it:

*As* the eyes *of slaves look to the hand of their master, as*
the eyes *of a maid look to the hand of her mistress . . .*
*(Psalm 123:2, emphasis added).*

In the ancient world, a servant closely watched the hands of
the master. With only a hand gesture, the master would signal for
a specific servant and indicate the kind of service required. For
this system to work, servants had to keep their eyes fixed on the
master's hands. In the same way, you can be an effective servant
by scanning to see the needs of others and keeping your mind
tuned to Jesus' high calling to lay down your life for another.

Let's move this discussion from theory to practice with
some examples of servant leadership in the military. Two soldiers, Mark and Alex, roomed together while attending technical training. Halfway through the course, Mark was excelling
and was one of the best in the class. His roommate, Alex, was
struggling with the work. Alex thought he could pass the course,
but it was going to take a lot of study and hard work. One Friday
afternoon, the First Sergeant posted the weekend duty roster.
Alex was scheduled for weekend work detail. Everyone was
assigned to that detail periodically, and it was Alex's turn. Normally, this would not have been a problem, but this weekend it
sent Alex into a panic. A big test was scheduled for Monday, and
Alex needed every available minute that weekend to study. Alex
went back to his room and shared his problem with Mark.
Remember, a servant is one who sees a need and meets it, without being asked and without expecting reward.

Mark saw a need and met it. He knew his roommate needed
extra time to study that weekend, so he obtained permission to
take Alex's place on the duty roster. Mark saw a need he could
meet, and he followed through with action.

Mark and Alex were the same rank. Mark's service was
about need, not position. It was not Mark's "position" to serve

his roommate. It was a need, seen and solved, without being asked, without expecting reward. If you're looking, you will see opportunities to serve time and again in the military. Your service to others is limited only by a failure to observe and an unwillingness to act.

What about officers and NCOs? Are they expected to serve, too? Yes, and their ability to serve increases with additional authority. A leader serves subordinates by (nothing new here!) seeing the needs and meeting them, without being asked and without expecting reward.

Here's another example. A large group of airmen was preparing aircraft for an upcoming mission. They were working long hours in miserable weather conditions, most of the time without complaining. The nearest place to get a hot meal was four miles away. The shuttle bus that transported the airmen to their dorms and the dining facility ran only once an hour. Many of the airmen skipped meals or snacked on food they brought with them. The wing commander, a senior officer, saw a need and used his power and authority to meet it. He ordered a mobile dining facility to be positioned within walking distance of the airmen's workplace. He provided hot meals and a warm shelter. By seeing the need and meeting it, the commander served his subordinates.

Remember this: Serving is not limited to a lower-ranking person helping a higher-ranking person. That is just one of several possibilities. People of equal rank can see a need and meet it, as in the example of Mark and Alex, and people of higher rank can meet the needs of subordinates, as in the second example. *There is no limit to the good that can be done if you don't care who gets the credit!*

## AMPLE OPPORTUNITIES

People in the military face many challenges, even hardships. Stress attacks from a number of fronts—rigorous training, intense inspections and evaluations, pressure to continually improve—not to mention the unique stress of combat. Add to that the struggle to raise a family, stick to a budget, keep the car running, and put food on the table. With all of these pressures, most people appreciate a shoulder to lean on, someone to pray for them, an encouraging word, and an occasional helping hand. Whether at work, in your neighborhood, or in a fellowship of believers, there are many needs to be met. A person who helps lift the load for others can make a big difference in someone's life.

Here are some ways you could serve the people around you:
➤ Provide a meal for a family with a new baby.
➤ Give someone money to help with their bills.
➤ Visit a sick or wounded comrade in the hospital.
➤ Carry a backpack for a person who is exhausted or injured.
➤ Take someone's duty shift or unpleasant task when you are better able to bear that load.

## CONTAGIOUS SERVICE

Serving others is the practical daily evidence of Christ in us. We follow Jesus' example when we choose to serve others, to meet their needs, and to help them work through their challenges. The concept of serving, voluntarily, is foreign to our culture, even to our nature. Yet when we see it in action, we realize how powerful it is. As we willingly and cheerfully serve, meeting the needs we see around us, our acts and attitude become contagious. The example we set influences others. Eventually, a workplace, even an entire organization, can be significantly altered by the efforts of a few to meet the needs of others.

*Carry each other's burdens, and in this way you will fulfill the law of Christ (Galatians 6:2).*

**SUMMARY**

⊕ For a Christian, serving is not an option; it's a requirement.

⊕ As a member of the military, you are already experienced in serving. The words "service" and "military" go hand in hand.

⊕ There are many opportunities to serve others in the military.

⊕ Serving starts in the heart and is powered by the eyes.

⊕ Service can be to peers, subordinates, or supervisors. Rank should not limit your service.

⊕ The higher your position, the greater your power to serve.

# Pursuing Excellence

*People were overwhelmed with amazement. "He has done everything well," they said (Mark 7:37a).*

SUPPOSE THAT YOU NEED AN OPERATION. Before surgery, you are given an opportunity to tour the operating room and examine the instruments that will be used. You're glad to see how clean and sterile the room is. The doctors and nurses also appear "scrubbed" and clean. However, as you examine the scalpels, needles, and other instruments that will be used inside of you, you notice specks of dried blood, corrosion, and dust. Some even have mold growing on them! Would you proceed with the surgery?

When it comes to the important issues of life, little things—especially *internal* things—become very important. A little mold makes a huge difference when the highest standards are required.

As a member of the military, you are held to a high standard of behavior and character. A country desires and requires its military force to be made up of reliable, virtuous warriors. A powerful and well-trained army becomes a danger to its nation if it allows its standards to be lowered, if it ceases to pursue excellence in duty and character. Soldiers who are self-centered and shoddy in their performance diminish their army's capability.

## PERFORMANCE VS. CHARACTER

Chapter 4 discussed the importance of doing your work well the first time, all the time. The way you work and the degree of quality you strive for reflect the kind of person you are. When you pursue excellence on the job, you contribute to the strength of your unit. The excellent worker does not need to be prodded to perform but works diligently and cooperates with others, even when unsupervised. Warriors who pursue excellence finish their tasks on time. These are standards the military attempts to ingrain into its warriors to make the military effective and reliable. But a soldier can perform to these standards and still lack virtue. Excellence is sometimes associated only with work performance (quality and quantity). But excellence applies to matters of character, as well.

Consider the "performance vs. character" disconnect in this example. A pastor performs more weddings, funerals, and baptisms than any other clergyman in town. He preaches three times on Sunday and once on Wednesday. He visits people in hospitals and orphanages. In short, his outward performance is commendable. But he has a couple of detracting spots in his character. Outside of the pulpit, he uses profane words in day-to-day conversation. He has also been unfaithful to his wife. All of his excellent production is tainted by a few vices. Does it matter? Just like the clean room with dirty tools, a little dirt spoils it all. The preacher in this example demonstrates excellence in job performance but not in character. In his profession, that is a glaring discrepancy.

Consider also the airline pilot who was known for his exceptional flying skills. He was in the top 95th percentile of all the pilots in the industry. He had natural flying ability and made smoother landings than anyone in the business. He had only one small flaw, and not even a moral one. He often stayed up late watching TV. Consequently, he was usually very sleepy when he showed up to fly. He knew he needed to be alert to be responsible for the hundreds of lives in his care, but he did not exercise self-control in his late-night TV watching. On a few occasions, he actually dozed off while flying an airplane filled with passengers. His copilot roused him and threatened to report his poor performance. Knowing this about the pilot, would you want to fly on his airplane?

There are jobs in which even a little carelessness or lack of discipline is a grave danger. There are professions that demand virtue as an integral part of the job. The military is one of those professions.

## CHARACTERISTICS OF EXCELLENCE

The military points the way toward on-the-job excellence, but the pursuit of consistent character excellence, on and off duty, is a personal journey. Notice the word "journey." Virtue is not a destination. There are no graduates of "virtue school." The road to character excellence is a pathway that leads to increasingly higher standards of behavior. While virtue impacts your work, it must extend into all areas of your life. Excellence is about having one kind of character in all circumstances.

Virtuous living originated in the character of God. God created us in His image. When we sinned, we lost the perfection of character that God intended for us. In the redemptive process, He desires to build virtue and character back into us so we will be like Him again.

> *But just as he [God] who called you is holy, so be holy in all you do; for it is written: "Be holy, because I am holy"* *(1 Peter 1:15–16).*

What makes a person virtuous? What kinds of character are needed for your work in the military? It's impossible to describe them all, but let's examine some of the primary components of character and the implications for our behavior. Consider the traits that follow, one at a time, and the accompanying Scripture passages. Then ask yourself: "Am I pursuing this virtue in my life? If not, why not? Do I practice this character trait on duty but violate it other times? What can I do to begin the journey toward virtuous character in this area?"

### Honesty
" 'Do not steal. Do not lie. Do not deceive one another' " (Leviticus 19:11).

Honesty (sometimes called *integrity*) forms the bedrock of trust. When your supervisor knows you always tell the truth, he relies on you. If he supervises someone who occasionally lies, he can never fully depend on that person. There are only two possibilities with integrity: You either have it or you don't. It doesn't come in various shades of black and white. There is no such thing as a "white lie" or "bending the truth." Either you tell the truth all the time, or you lack integrity. Sound simple? The *principle* is simple. Following it without wavering is difficult. If several of your coworkers have already falsified a written report, it's tough to stand alone and report the truth on your version of the report. Tough, but necessary.

*A truthful witness saves lives, but a false witness is deceitful (Proverbs 14:25).*

*A false witness will not go unpunished, and he who pours out lies will not go free (Proverbs 19:5).*

A soldier who lies violates the Uniform Code of Military Justice (UCMJ; the special code of law that governs military people) and violates the trust of others. He also violates the laws of God. Though he may be punished for the lie under the authority of the UCMJ, his ability to regain trust is damaged. What is easily lost can take years to regain.

Developing excellence of character is a journey, but integrity is not. You must decide, once and for always, to be honest in all you say and do. From your first day in basic training to your last day on active duty (and beyond), be unswerving in your commitment to always be 100-percent truthful.

### Diligence

*Lazy hands make a man poor, but diligent hands bring wealth (Proverbs 10:4).*

*"His master replied, 'Well done, good and faithful servant! You have been faithful with a few things; I will put you in charge of many things. Come and share your master's happiness!' " (Matthew 25:23).*

In the book of Proverbs, diligence is contrasted with laziness. Diligent soldiers fulfill the command as well as the intent of the commander. They complete the whole task as quickly as possible, meeting or exceeding the requirements every time and without being asked. Do you know *anybody* like that? Few people work at being this diligent, but it is a behavior commended by the Bible.

Jesus told the story of a master who was pleased by the servant who faithfully carried out the small responsibilities he was given. Diligence begins with small tasks. As you prove your diligence in small tasks, you distinguish yourself as an excellent worker, one who goes above and beyond the call of duty. Diligence thrives out of the spotlight. It requires a commitment to be thorough and effective regardless of who is watching. The principle applies to the lone rifleman in a foxhole as well as the skipper of a ship.

Diligence is almost always rewarded. Look at this promise from the Bible:

*The sluggard craves and gets nothing, but the desires of the diligent are fully satisfied (Proverbs 13:4).*

If you come from a background of laziness, expecting others to do things for you, it will take time to change. Diligence is a learned character trait best taught by modeling. When you see it in others, you appreciate it and begin to duplicate it. Others then see it in you, and the process continues. Diligence would come easier if you looked at your supervisor each day and saw the face of Jesus. If you thought you were working for your Lord and Savior, wouldn't it affect your attitude and work? That is what the writer of Colossians says you are to do—serve as if Jesus really *is* your supervisor.

*Whatever you do, work at it with all your heart, as working for the Lord, not for men (Colossians 3:23).*

Ask yourself these questions, "Would anyone consider me a diligent worker? Do I . . .
➤ Start and complete tasks quickly?
➤ Pick hard and dirty jobs when I have a choice, or do I always leave those for others if possible?
➤ Continue to read and study to learn more about my work?
➤ Expand my job to fill up the time available, or do I finish it quickly and look for more work?
➤ Have a clear conscience at the end of the day, knowing I have done my best?"

What can you do to become more diligent? One of the best ways is to be around someone who is already good at it. Seek to be around people who are good examples of diligence and quality workmanship. Start today, the next time you go on shift. Consider how you have done your work in the past, and ask yourself, "What one or two things could I do better today than I did yesterday?"

### Humility

*Young men, in the same way be submissive to those who are older. All of you, clothe yourselves with humility toward one another, because, "God opposes the proud but gives grace to the humble." Humble yourselves, therefore, under God's mighty hand, that he may lift you up in due time (1 Peter 5:5–6).*

This passage starts by singling out young men, but then it instructs everyone to exercise humility. God opposes the proud. Do you want God as your opponent? Then guard against developing the common, unholy trait of pride.

But aren't we supposed to be proud, at least about some things? The Marines actually use this in their slogan: "The few, the proud." Some words in English have more than one possible meaning. Pride is one of those words. Webster's dictionary gives two definitions: *1) Glory or delight* and *2) Inordinate self-esteem*. The military encourages the first; our culture encourages the second.

In the 1960s, boxer Cassius Clay (a.k.a. Mohammed Ali) made quite a scene yelling at the top of his voice to the TV cameras, "I am the greatest!" It was novel and interesting back then because no other sports figures at the time were so self-aggrandizing. Today that boastful attitude has become an art form! The sports world is full of flashy moves in the end zone and all kinds of "look-at-me" gestures.

Is it possible to be a highly skilled, accomplished warrior and remain humble? Absolutely! In 1872, a man named Phillips Brooks said this:

"The true way to be humble is not to stoop until you are smaller than yourself, but to stand at your real height against some higher nature that will show you what the real smallness of your greatness is."

You can strive to "be all that you can be" and still remain humble. Humility is not about being less than you could be; it's about realizing that your abilities and strengths are gifts from God. The opposite of humility is not pride, it's ungratefulness. Inordinate self-esteem (the bad kind of pride) comes from a failure to acknowledge the contribution of God and other people in your success.

Surrounded by a world that encourages flagrant bragging, it's not easy to stay humble. The world does not always reward humility, but it is commended and rewarded by God now and eternally.

*Do nothing out of selfish ambition or vain conceit, but in humility consider others better than yourselves. Each of you should look not only to your own interests, but also to the interests of others. Your attitude should be the same as that of Christ Jesus (Philippians 2:3–5).*

### Control of the tongue
*Do not revile the king even in your thoughts, or curse the rich in your bedroom, because a bird of the air may carry your words, and a bird on the wing may report what you say (Ecclesiastes 10:20).*

OK, a bird may not literally carry your words through the air, but the point is that what you think eventually finds its way into your attitudes and speech. Of highest importance to anyone in the military is loyalty to supervisors and leaders. Nothing diminishes a warrior as much as thoughtless criticism of a unit or person. It is easy to get caught up in the "ain't it awful" spirit, mindlessly assassinating the character of others. It's easy to get swept into criticism of the various people in your unit. Fact-sharing soon becomes criticism, with each speaker trying to impress the group by adding additional insight on the flaws of this person or that policy.

The New Testament book of James gives this caution about the tongue:

> *Likewise the tongue is a small part of the body, but it makes great boasts. Consider what a great forest is set on fire by a small spark. The tongue also is a fire, a world of evil among the parts of the body. It corrupts the whole person, sets the whole course of his life on fire, and is itself set on fire by hell (James 3:5–6).*

The tongue can drop "sparks of fire" that spread, leaving behind unimaginable destruction. If you want to be regarded as a true professional and an excellent warrior, refrain from criticism, slander, and foolish speech.

> *Do not let any unwholesome talk come out of your mouths, but only what is helpful for building others up according to their needs, that it may benefit those who listen (Ephesians 4:29).*

### *Courage*

> *"Be strong and very courageous. Be careful to obey all the law my servant Moses gave you; do not turn from it to the right or to the left, that you may be successful wherever you go. . . . Have I not commanded you? Be strong and courageous. Do not be terrified; do not be discouraged, for the LORD your God will be with you wherever you go" (Joshua 1:7, 9).*

Courage is one of the fundamental character traits required of warriors. Sometimes you don't even know you have it until you need it. The history of warfare is filled with stories of unlikely soldiers who, at a desperate point in battle, demonstrated amazing personal courage. Courage is the part of you that sees the danger but moves to action anyway.

Perhaps the best illustration of this is the biblical example of young David facing the giant Goliath (1 Samuel 17). Goliath was a fearsome warrior whose size and unquestioned strength had caused the army of Israel to hunker down in fear. David was not blind to Goliath's size. His estimate of Goliath's strength was no less than others. But David felt that Goliath was an affront to God and believed, for that reason, that he could be defeated with God's help. David recounted instances when he had defeated sizeable, worthy opponents (see 1 Samuel 17:34, particularly) with God's help. David's courage, and ours, is fueled by focusing not just on the threat, but on the possibility of victory by the power of God.

As a Christian, you can find courage in God's promise to be with you and give you strength.

*"So do not fear, for I am with you; do not be dismayed, for I am your God. I will strengthen you and help you; I will uphold you with my righteous right hand. All who rage against you will surely be ashamed and disgraced; those who oppose you will be as nothing and perish" (Isaiah 41:10–11).*

Courage is not just reserved for battlefields. It takes courage to do the right thing all of the time. It takes courage to daily choose the path of excellence. Sometimes the world will applaud your attempts to live a righteous and blameless life; other times it will mock. Being courageous in your daily decisions, often in the face of opposition, is only possible when your eyes are fixed on God. Consider Moses' example:

> *By faith he left Egypt, not fearing the king's anger; he perse-vered because he saw him who is invisible (Hebrews 11:27).*

Only with an accurate perspective on life, death, judgment, and eternity can you consistently make good decisions and act in a way that pleases God. Little, daily courageous decisions prepare you for the larger "battlefield" confrontations you will face.

## CHOOSE TO PURSUE EXCELLENCE

God wants our lives to increasingly reflect the virtue that is innate in His own character. Resolve every day to be God's soldier. Choose to do right, to tell the truth, and to maintain a clear conscience before God and man.

> *Be on your guard; stand firm in the faith; be men of courage; be strong (1 Corinthians 16:13).*

 **SUMMARY**

⊕ Excellence means becoming all that God intends for us to be.
⊕ Growing in excellence requires developing our character.
⊕ Godly character calls for honesty, diligence, humility, control of the tongue, and courage.
⊕ Growth in these characteristics is a daily, purposeful journey.

# Family Matters

*If anyone does not provide for his relatives, and especially for his immediate family, he has denied the faith and is worse than an unbeliever (1 Timothy 5:8).*

YOUR FAMILY MATTERS TO GOD. You are responsible to raise your children in a way that honors God and helps them become responsible, productive members of society. Can you successfully fulfill this duty in the military environment? The underlying concerns embodied in this question include:

➤ What effect will frequent moves have on your children?
➤ Will you be able to control the environment in which your kids develop?
➤ What will be the effect of not having extended family members nearby?
➤ What churches and Sunday schools will be available?
➤ What kind of schools will your children attend?

All parents have some of these apprehensions, but life in the military adds even more challenges—frequent moves, family separation, and the absence of extended-family support. Given these conditions, is it possible to raise "normal," well-adjusted kids in the military?

The answer is an unequivocal "yes"! In fact, some features of military life actually provide *greater* opportunities for the growth and stability of your family. Your children have the potential to be stronger, more flexible, and more well-rounded because of your service in the military.

## GOD'S INSTRUCTIONS FOR PARENTS

Surprisingly, the Bible contains very few references on the important topic of raising children. The 66 books of the Old and New Testaments contain only a handful of verses that give instructions for child rearing. God recorded His plan for parenting in only a few verses. His Word is clear and concise. Perhaps it's not as complex as the volumes of new books on the subject make it seem. Perhaps there are a few underlying principles that make parenting, under any conditions, a relatively simple task.

The clearest principle for parents all over the world, in every kind of circumstance, is found in the Old Testament book of Deuteronomy:

> These commandments that I give you today are to be upon your hearts. Impress them on your children. Talk about them when you sit at home and when you walk along the road, when you lie down and when you get up. Tie them as symbols on your hands and bind them on your foreheads. Write them on the doorframes of your houses and on your gates (Deuteronomy 6:6–9).

The principle is this: *Integrate the teaching of God's Word into every activity of life.* That's it? Yes! We're told to daily educate our children in God's commandments, principles, guidelines, and wisdom, found in the Bible, using the circumstances of life as our teaching tools. This is a universal principle. It applied to Old Testament Jews and New Testament Christians, and it applies to military families today. It places the entire responsibility for raising and educating children on the shoulders of parents. It encourages a systematic, daily exposure of our children to the circumstances of life, measured against the yardstick of God's Word.

*My son, if you accept my words and store up my commands within you, turning your ear to wisdom and applying your heart to understanding, and if you call out for insight and cry aloud for understanding, and if you look for it as for silver and search for it as for hidden treasure, then you will understand the fear of the LORD and find the knowledge of God. For the LORD gives wisdom, and from his mouth come knowledge and understanding (Proverbs 2:1–6).*

## DEFINING WHAT'S NORMAL

As a parent, your goal is to teach your children that God is the Creator and Sustainer of all life, that He created each of us and has a design for us. Allow God to use the circumstances of life to help you shape, train, and prepare your kids for His service. Incidentally, this is not a process that ends after childhood. God expects us, as adults, to observe life, compare what we see with what God says about it, and adapt to His wisdom and ways.

God established the special organization known as "the family" to be a child's first classroom and the Bible to be the first textbook. Children learn to respond to the challenges of life in the same way their parents respond. Think about that for a minute. *Children do what they see their parents do.* For example, if you teach your children that going to church is important but your own attendance is sporadic, your children will probably duplicate your actions, not your teaching, when they get older.

As parents respond to challenges and difficulties, they teach their children "normal" behavior in that set of circumstances. If parents respond in a way that is honoring to God, children will naturally learn to connect the "normal" behavior with God's desire for them. They learn that God has something to say about the issues and decisions of their lives and that difficult circumstances provide exceptional opportunities to see God act.

*For the eyes of the LORD run to and fro throughout the whole earth, to show himself strong in the behalf of them whose heart is perfect toward Him (2 Chronicles 16:9a, KJV).*

God wants to act on behalf of those who trust Him. He wants to show Himself strong in the lives of those who obey Him. He wants to give victory over circumstances. To do this allows Him to receive glory and challenges unbelieving bystanders to consider the greatness of God.

## RESPONDING TO MILITARY CHANGES

Let's take this principle, *integrate the teaching of God into every activity of life,* and consider some applications to the specific challenges of military life. Parents are to teach this great principle by modeling it every day. The following table addresses two issues specific to military life. It gives two ways parents could react and what God has to say about it.

| Circumstance | Positive Reaction | Negative Reaction | What God Says |
|---|---|---|---|
| Moving to a new location | Great opportunity, new possibilities | Fear of the unknown, disruption | I will be with you in all of life's most difficult events. (Isaiah 43:2) |
| Family separation | A time when God can minister to the family in a special way | A perilous time accompanied by loneliness, sense of loss | I am able to make good come, even from evil circumstances. (Genesis 50:20) |

Identify the hard issues in your family's lives, learn what God has to say about them, and make your own chart like this one. Examine your own negative and positive feelings, and discover the promises and principles God has established for such circumstances. This requires familiarity with God's Word. God wants to bless families as they seek to follow Him and obey His Word.

*Keep his decrees and commands, which I am giving you today, so that it may go well with you and your children after you and that you may live long in the land the LORD your God gives you for all time (Deuteronomy 4:40).*

This exercise in not about the "power of positive thinking." It's not about forcing yourself to feel good about bad things or closing your eyes to the real challenges and difficulties of life. Rather, it is allowing God to be God in every circumstance. It is obtaining the power to go through difficult circumstances victoriously—not in a mindless, sugar-coated way, but in a courageous, God-empowered way. God wants us to depend on Him. He allows difficult circumstances to come our way so we can develop our "faith muscles."

*This is what the LORD says: "Let not the wise man boast of his wisdom or the strong man boast of his strength or the rich man boast of his riches, but let him who boasts boast about this: that he understands and knows me, that I am the LORD, who exercises kindness, justice and righteousness on earth, for in these I delight," declares the LORD (Jeremiah 9:23–24, emphasis added).*

God gives us wisdom, strength, and riches. But in the "crunch," He wants us to turn to Him, not to the meager resources we call our own. As parents do this, they model the

behavior that pleases God and leads to a fulfilled and fruitful life.
The nomadic lifestyle of military families is different from
that of most families. The differences can be viewed as good or
bad, as opportunities or hardships.

| Military Life Circumstance | Opportunity | Hardship |
|---|---|---|
| Change schools often | Make new friends | Move away from old friends |
| No home church | New pastors, new perspective and insight | Changed patterns of worship; disrupted "comfort zone" |
| Live in faraway places | Broader education; experience new customs and food; see new sights; gain broader perspective on life | Separation from extended family; subjected to new customs and food |
| Military housing | Live in a "gated community"; added security and support | Not able to live in "my own" house; must keep yard and house to military standards |
| Temporary absence of military parent | Children take on new level of responsibility, learn to depend on God sooner and for more areas of their lives | Less leadership at home; one parent bears the load alone; children suffer loss |
| Regimented lifestyle | Learn to thrive in a community; learn social responsibility; find pleasure in group activities | Can't do my own thing, must adapt to others; hard to be unique or by myself; must conform to community standards |

Children will respond to these and other circumstances in the way they see their parents respond. If the parents view the unique features of military life as a positive challenge, as a means to growth and development, children will generally feel the same way. This may not always be easy. Continually ask God to show you how this circumstance will benefit you and your family. Ask Him to let you see things as He sees them.

Military parents must walk in faith. If God has called and led you to a career in the military, trust Him to meet your needs and the needs of your children.

## DRILL-SERGEANT PARENTING

Now for a word of caution. It is important for the parent who is in the military (sometimes it's both parents) to distinguish family life from military life. Your family may live in base housing, attend Department of Defense schools, and use military theaters, stores, and recreation facilities, but *they are not in the military*. It's easy to think that the family can be run like a military unit. As a soldier, you spend most of your day giving and taking orders, responding instantly when necessary. You may return home with the same expectations for your family.

Remember the VonTrapp family in the movie *The Sound of Music*? Captain VonTrapp infused (and abused!) his naval experience into his children. He ordered them to attention, then each responded by taking one step forward, announcing his or her name, then returning to attention in line with the other children. This sort of instant, rigid obedience may be necessary in the military, but it's not the way to raise a loving family. Children need discipline, but it doesn't need to follow the military's model.

## SETTING THE TONE

Whether your military family thrives or deteriorates is largely up to you, the parent. Your attitude and perspective will set the tone for the rest of your family. You can raise a healthy family by seeing events from God's point of view and relying on His resources to equip your family for every challenge.

*"For I am the LORD, your God, who takes hold of your right hand and says to you, Do not fear; I will help you" (Isaiah 41:13).*

### SUMMARY

- ✦ The biblical principle of parenting is to integrate the teaching of God into every activity of life.
- ✦ The military offers families unique opportunities and challenges, which can be viewed as either good or bad.
- ✦ The attitudes you demonstrate will help your children define what is "normal."
- ✦ As God demonstrates His faithfulness to meet your family's needs, He strengthens your character and faith.
- ✦ The military offers incredible opportunities for your children, such as education, travel, and growth.
- ✦ You may be in the military, but your children aren't. Be sure you don't treat them like fellow soldiers.

# Part III:
# The Victorious Christian Life

THE MILITARY PROFESSION, by its very nature, is dangerous. But living an undisciplined, uncontrolled, and unprotected life is even more dangerous. Part III will describe the major traps and dangers that have tripped up others in the past. These threats are not invincible. If you take time to prepare yourself before you confront them, you can achieve spiritual victory.

The time-honored principles of war presented in Chapter 20 will help you apply your military warfare skills to the spiritual warfare you face, serving as a concise handbook for spiritual victory.

Consider carefully the teaching in the following chapters, be aware of the enemies of your soul, and seek, by the power of God, to live the victorious Christian life each day as you serve in the military.

# Fellowship

*Two are better than one, because they have a good return
for their work: If one falls down, his friend can help him
up. But pity the man who falls and has no one to help him
up! . . . Though one may be overpowered, two can defend
themselves. A cord of three strands is not quickly broken
(Ecclesiastes 4:9–10, 12).*

THE CHRISTIAN'S AIM SHOULD BE to live a fruitful, productive life and finish well. At the end of your life, you want to be able to say, like the apostle Paul, "I have fought the good fight, I have finished the race, I have kept the faith" (2 Timothy 4:7). Few of life's achievements are accomplished alone, and that includes living a fruitful and victorious life. The author of Ecclesiastes states it so well: "Pity the man who falls and has no one to help him up!" (Ecclesiastes 4:10).

Every soldier needs a partner. In combat aviation, this is referred to as a "wingman," someone to "check your six." No soldier would enter a battlefield alone. You need others to cover your blind spots, to provide protection on your flanks, as well as to your rear. The idea of mutual protection is self-evident in combat, but it is often overlooked in spiritual warfare.

*For our struggle is not against flesh and blood, but
against the rulers, against the authorities, against the*

*powers of this dark world and against the spiritual forces of evil in the heavenly realms (Ephesians 6:12).*

You are engaged in a perpetual war, raging in the heavenly realms, and you cannot expect to last long on that battlefield if you are isolated and alone.

Samson, one of the great judges of Israel, provided a poignant example of the dangers of being alone. Throughout the pages that describe Samson's life, there is no mention of a friend or ally. In the beginning, that seemed to be OK. Samson was strong, tough, and effective in battle, a real "man's man." Using his God-given, supernatural strength, he triumphed alone. But even the most powerful people need friends and partners. If Samson had *just one friend* looking out for him, his life would have turned out differently. Instead, he began living immorally, eventually becoming involved with a woman who would take his strength, his eyes, and his freedom. He ended up as a slave (Judges 16).

Do *you* have a friend who knows you well enough to realize when you are in spiritual or moral danger? Is there someone in your life who could keep you from making poor decisions in your weakest areas?

## IT ONLY TAKES TWO

Nothing knocks you down quicker than being the only Christian in a group of nonbelievers. Nothing cools the bright flame of your spiritual ember more than being isolated from other fervent followers of Jesus.

One of the proven principles of war is "mass." The principle of mass is to gather on the battlefield a force of manpower and equipment that overwhelms the enemy. This principle has direct application to spiritual warfare, with one important difference. Using this principle, you might think that to stand strong as a Christian, you need a large group of people for strength and protection. The math works a bit differently in the spiritual realm. Jesus stated it this way:

*"Again, I tell you that if two of you on earth agree about anything you ask for, it will be done for you by my Father in heaven. For where two or three come together in my name, there am I with them" (Matthew 18:19–20, emphasis added).*

Jesus promised His presence and power to a "group" as small as two! The equation looks like this:

**Two people + Jesus = God's attention/answers to prayer**

In spiritual warfare, a "mass" can be just two people, along with Jesus. This is a good thing, because in many military units, the number of committed, active Christians is small. Sometimes there is only one. That fact should not dampen your fervor or faithfulness to God. Jesus promises to be with you in a group as small as two or three. If you are the only Christian in your unit, link up with someone from another unit. Or find support through an e-mail buddy or pen pal. However you work it out, get connected to another person who is actively following Jesus.

If you are married, you may look to your spouse as that partner and protector. This is one of the great benefits that comes with marriage—the lifelong partnership and accountability to another person. However, military service often requires separation between marriage partners. Any time you know you're going to be away from your spouse, for a weekend or a year, you should be thinking about finding another accountability partner to help you and to protect your blind spots.

## CONNECTING WITH OTHERS

There are *no* successful "Lone Rangers" in the Christian life! (And even the Lone Ranger had Tonto to look out for him!) They don't exist. There are also no "undercover agent" or "special forces" Christians dropped alone behind enemy lines. God blesses and protects us through fellowship with other believers. In many ways, we are like sheep. God encourages us to "flock together" and keep our eyes on the Shepherd. If you do these two things, you can expect His protection and blessing on your life. If you don't, you can expect to be devoured by your enemy. The Bible describes Satan as a roaring lion, seeking those he can devour (1 Peter 5:8). Lions look for the lone sheep, the injured or the straggler.

You will be very vulnerable to this "lone-sheep" attack when transitioning from one assignment to the next. It is essential at each new assignment, on each new job, aboard each new ship, to identify yourself as a Christian early on—within the first week—and quickly find others of like heart. You can do this by mentioning your faith in appropriate conversations and places. Check bulletin boards for Bible study groups and chapel services. Chaplains can be another good resource. They are tuned in to the spiritual condition and needs of their soldiers and can help you identify opportunities for local fellowship.

### BENEFITS OF FELLOWSHIP

The fellowship of one or more other Christians provides for you in these important areas:

➤ **Protection.** You help watch out for each other, holding each other accountable to live like Jesus in every facet of your lives.

➤ **Partnership.** Nothing lifts your spirits as much as knowing you are not alone, that you have a partner who will help you bear up under pressure.

➤ **Prayer.** Jesus said if two people agree on anything, it shall be done. You apply the power of Almighty God to your circumstances when you pray for and with other people.

**Protection + Partnership + Prayer = Spiritual Victory**

### THE IMPORTANCE OF ACCOUNTABILITY

Fellowship with other believers can occur in a worship service, a Bible study, at a coffee house, or in a dorm room. When we meet with other believers, we share stories about what God has been doing in our lives. We exchange prayer requests and pray for one another. Sometimes we sing praise together. Often, as in worship services, someone will teach or preach. When we fellowship with others, we come away encouraged, strengthened, and more prepared for spiritual battle.

But it's possible to enjoy fellowship with other believers without letting anyone see the true condition of your soul. That's where small group, or even one-on-one, accountability comes in. The prophet Jeremiah wrote, "The heart is deceitful above all things, and desperately wicked: who can know it?" (Jeremiah 17:9, KJV). We can give the appearance that we are doing well, but we may be struggling internally with temptation that no one knows about. Being accountable means being open, giving permission to ask tough, direct questions, and agreeing to be totally honest with one another. This is hardball! It's tough to be this open and candid. It means that our accountability partners can ask questions about every facet of our life, from how we use our time and money to the personal details of our thought life.

When we know we must give account to others about our thoughts and actions, we are much more careful about our decisions. This is the value of accountability. Here are some suggestions to set up a healthy and mutually beneficial accountability partnership:

➤ Pick one or two people of the same sex, whom you trust and respect for their character.
➤ Develop a few questions that you agree to ask each other. Focus on areas in which each of you struggle.
➤ Meet once a week (or more, if necessary) to ask each other questions and to talk about your lives.
➤ Confess sin, tempting situations, and struggles; then pray for one another.

*Therefore put on the full armor of God, so that when the day of evil comes, you may be able to stand your ground, and after you have done everything, to stand (Ephesians 6:13).*

"After we have done *everything.*" We put on the full armor of God by participating in fellowship groups, worshipping with others, and sharing our lives with one another. But we also need to do everything we can to stand our ground in the day of temptation. That means banding together with a few others to protect and pray for each other.

## CHOOSING FELLOWSHIP

The choice to either be a loner or to tie into a group of other Christians is yours to make. Expect a hard road if you choose to walk alone.

If you want to live an increasingly victorious life, *you* must take the initiative to seek fellowship and maintain contact with other believers at each duty station.

*And let us consider how we may spur one another on toward love and good deeds. Let us not give up meeting together, as some are in the habit of doing, but let us encourage one another—and all the more as you see the Day approaching (Hebrews 10:24–25).*

## SUMMARY

✤ Fellowship is the foundation for a victorious Christian life.

✤ Fellowship incorporates many kinds of activities, such as singing, praying, and listening to a message.

✤ Accountability is a key component of fellowship.

✤ In an accountability relationship, we give one or two others permission to ask hard questions about the issues in our lives.

✤ Each of us needs to care for and protect other Christians through committed relationships.

# The Enemy Within

*So I find this law at work: When I want to do good, evil is right there with me (Romans 7:21).*

AS THE EASTERN SKY BRIGHTENED with the first rays of sunrise, General George Armstrong Custer peered through his telescope toward the valley of the Little Bighorn River. From his perch atop the rocky Crow's Nest peak, he could see for miles to the north and west. His scouts told him they had seen smoke from cooking fires and huge herds of horses in the valley. Custer, however, saw nothing, even with the aid of the telescope. He was not convinced that his enemies, the Sioux, were nearby. Even if they were, he was unaware of their numbers. Descending from the ridge, he divided his men, sending them in different directions. The result became one of history's best-known defeats. By the end of the day, Custer and every soldier riding with him was killed. The Sioux, along with allied tribes, outnumbered Custer's forces by at least four to one! Historians have debated the reasons for this stunning defeat, but on one point they all agree: Custer sent a *divided force* to face an *enemy he knew little about.* He did not know how many he would face or even where they were. God warns His children against making this same mistake.

## FACING OUR INTERNAL ENEMY

It is easy to ignore or underestimate one of our greatest, nearest foes—our own sinful nature! What does this old nature look like? It's our innate desire to go our own way and act contrary to what we know God desires. When we turn to Jesus for salvation, we receive forgiveness for our sins and stand "clean" before a holy God. We receive a new nature that is attentive to the Spirit of God, but the old nature remains.

If we underestimate the power and destructiveness of our sin nature, we treat it too gently, even feeding its desires. Our old nature rages against the new creation we are in Christ. In the book of Galatians, Paul explained it this way:

> *For the whole energy of the lower nature is set against the Spirit, while the whole power of the Spirit is contrary to the lower nature. Here is the conflict, and that is why you are not able to do what you want to do (Galatians 5:17, PHILLIPS).*

Writing to the Roman church, Paul graphically expressed his own internal struggle:

> *So I find this law at work: When I want to do good, evil is right there with me. For in my inner being I delight in God's law; but I see another law at work in the members of my body, waging war against the law of my mind and making me a prisoner of the law of sin at work within my members. What a wretched man I am! Who will rescue me from this body of death? (Romans 7:21–24).*

You've probably heard the phrase, "We have found the enemy, and it is us!" Although it's meant to be funny, it characterizes our human nature more than we'd like to think. Seeing the complete corruption of man, God sent a flood to purge the world of its rebellious pursuit.

*The LORD saw how great man's wickedness on the earth
had become, and that every inclination of the thoughts of
his heart was only evil all the time. The LORD was grieved
that he had made man on the earth, and his heart was
filled with pain. So the LORD said, "I will wipe mankind,
whom I have created, from the face of the earth" (Genesis
6:5–7a).*

These are strong words: *"Every inclination* of the thoughts of
his heart was only *evil all the time."* This is a description of a
heart beyond minor repair. It is a fallen nature past simple
reform. Away from the presence of God, man's heart inflates
with selfish ego. It works at perfecting evil. It prevents its own
sensitivity and dulls its own conscience to any word from God.
Jeremiah, prophet of Israel, said this about the heart:

*The heart is deceitful above all things and beyond cure.
Who can understand it? (Jeremiah 17:9).*

To this dire estimate of man's inner self, Jesus added His
assessment:

*He went on: "What comes out of a man is what makes
him 'unclean.' For from within, out of men's hearts, come
evil thoughts, sexual immorality, theft, murder, adultery,
greed, malice, deceit, lewdness, envy, slander, arrogance
and folly. All these evils come from inside and make a
man 'unclean' " (Mark 7:20–23).*

Make no mistake about it. The source of evil that flows from
our minds, mouths, and actions is *our own heart!* Picture a military unit in formation, hundreds of soldiers standing side by
side, ready for battle. Now imagine that one soldier in five is

actually an agent for the opposing army. No general would send such an infiltrated army into combat! Yet this is the picture we would see if we could peer into the depths of our own heart.

As Christians, God has given us a new nature that responds to the prompting of the Holy Spirit and the commands of Jesus. But the old sin nature still lives within us, infiltrating our being. It yearns to fulfill fleshly cravings. It wants to be nourished and exalted. The old nature wants to sit in the commander's seat giving orders to the rest of the body. If we fail to comprehend the proximity and power of this spiritual enemy, like Custer we will be defeated. If, on the other hand, we properly identify the enemy's location and strength, we can prepare for and win the battle against the old nature inside of us.

## LOCATING THE ENEMY

*The Enemy Below,* an exciting naval-combat movie, tells the story of a destroyer and a submarine engaged in a deadly search to find and destroy one another. After a cat-and-mouse chase in the North Atlantic, the submarine dives deep and stops, silencing all machinery. The silence causes the destroyer to lose contact with the submarine. The destroyer also comes to a complete and silent stop. The two adversaries listen for any sound that would jeopardize the enemy's position. The camera then focuses on a sailor who lowers a fishing line over the side of the destroyer, hoping to catch some fish to feed the crew. The camera follows the fishing line slowly down, underwater, descending straight below the hull of the destroyer . . . and there is the submarine! Separated by only a few hundred feet of water, the enemy ships rest one on top of the other.

So it is with our new and old nature. Our new spiritual nature operates on the surface, while the dangerous old nature lurks below. The book of Romans paints this picture of our "enemy below":

*I do not understand what I do. For what I want to do I do not do, but what I hate I do. . . . For what I do is not the good I want to do; no, the evil I do not want to do—this I keep on doing. Now if I do what I do not want to do, it is no longer I who do it, but it is sin living in me that does it. So I find this law at work: When I want to do good, evil is right there with me (Romans 7:15, 19–21).*

### "THE DEVIL MADE ME DO IT!"

Comedian Flip Wilson made this line, "The devil made me do it," famous, but he was not the first to use this excuse. It was first used in the Garden of Eden. Eve claimed it as the reason she disobeyed God. Blaming Satan may be a tempting excuse for our sinful behavior, but it's not a valid one. No one *made* Eve choose sin. *She* chose her own behavior. The book of James warns against the power of our old nature:

*But each one is tempted when,* by his own evil desire, *he is dragged away and enticed. Then, after desire has conceived, it gives birth to sin; and sin, when it is full-grown, gives birth to death (James 1:14–15, emphasis added).*

Human beings are born with the innate desire to sin. In fact, we are incapable of avoiding sin. Most men and women spend their early years nurturing and strengthening this sinful nature. The devil may *tempt* us to do evil, but our old nature delights to do the bidding of the tempter. When we invite Jesus to be Lord of our lives, He gives us a new nature, one that delights in doing the will of God. This gracious gift immediately ignites a struggle. When the new nature is given to a believer, the old nature doesn't just pack up and leave. It struggles desperately to maintain control over body, mind, and soul.

The Bible gives an excellent example of this struggle in the book of 2 Samuel. After disobedient King Saul was removed from the throne, his followers continued to fight against the newly anointed King David.

*The war between the house of Saul and the house of David lasted a long time. David grew stronger and stronger, while the house of Saul grew weaker and weaker (2 Samuel 3:1).*

This is a picture of what should happen in the life of a Christian. The new nature should grow "stronger and stronger" as the old nature grows "weaker and weaker."

### THE ENEMY'S DESIRES

When we turn our backs on God and assume we are no longer accountable to Him, the old nature is given full rein. John identifies the most prominent features of this in the book of 1 John:

*Do not love the world or anything in the world. If anyone loves the world, the love of the Father is not in him. For everything in the world—the cravings of sinful man, the lust of his eyes and the boasting of what he has and does—comes not from the Father but from the world (1 John 2:15–16).*

The old nature is very predictable; it wants more of everything except God! It seeks:
➤ Worldly values and philosophy
➤ Material possessions
➤ Sexual license
➤ Self-determination
➤ Fame and praise from people

People ruled by their sinful nature hope there will be no consequences, but they're never completely sure that there won't be some "final accounting" in the end. Therefore, they never really enjoy their self-declared independence and unbridled pursuit of pleasure.

You may shake your head at people ruled by their worldly cravings, but this same nature was the first ruler on the throne of your life, as well. Strong and unopposed, it directed your decisions and craved worldly pleasure. But you took an important step in changing that when you made Jesus Lord and Savior of your life. Now that you have the new nature in you, give Jesus His rightful place in your life and stop feeding the old nature.

### FINDING VICTORY

Custer fought his last battle on June 25, the middle of summer. Is that date significant? Yes, at least it was for the Plains Indians. Living off the land was difficult much of the year. One small area could not support many Indians, especially in the winter. Wild game for the Indians and forage for their ponies were scarce during winter months, so the tribes would split up. The Indians were at their worst during the winter but got stronger in the spring, when the tribes joined back together for companionship and mutual defense. The natural grassland flourished. The Indians and their horses ate well, achieving their maximum strength and capability in mid-summer. If Custer would have considered this, he might not have planned a June 25 attack.

If you continue to "feed" your old nature, it will remain strong. If you want victory in your life, follow the prompting of your new nature and put the old nature to death. This is how Paul instructed the Roman believers:

*In the same way, count yourselves dead to sin but alive to God in Christ Jesus. Therefore do not let sin reign in your mortal body so that you obey its evil desires. Do not offer the parts of your body to sin, as instruments of wickedness, but rather offer yourselves to God, as those who have been brought from death to life; and offer the parts of your body to him as instruments of righteousness (Romans 6:11–13).*

Instead of listening to the old nature and following its desires, listen to the new nature and fill your mind with the powerful Word of God. Listen to David's instructions in the book of Psalms:

*How can a young man keep his way pure? By living according to your word.... I have hidden your word in my heart that I might not sin against you (Psalm 119:9, 11).*

Think of it this way. Suppose you have two puppies in your backyard. Each has its own doghouse and food dish. As the puppies grow up, you notice one of them is vicious—growling, barking, and biting. It tries to eat the other dog's food as well as its own. In contrast, the second puppy is friendly, happy, and serves you faithfully. Then you realize that the one you feed the most controls the atmosphere of the backyard. Isn't it obvious which dog you should feed the most?

It's equally obvious which nature you should feed. The old nature is uncontrollable, constantly lusting for more and leading to painful consequences.

*For a man's ways are in full view of the LORD, and he examines all his paths. The evil deeds of a wicked man ensnare him; the cords of his sin hold him fast. He will die for lack of discipline, led astray by his own great folly (Proverbs 5:21–23).*

In the new nature, there is life. Which will you choose to follow? The first step in victory is to acknowledge the presence and power of the enemy within. Next, refrain from listening to the old nature. Instead, focus on daily nurturing the new nature, feeding on the Word of God, and listening to the Holy Spirit. Little by little, you will see the "dog" you don't feed weakening, and your new spiritual nature prevailing.

 **SUMMARY**

⊕ When you received Christ, you gained a new spiritual nature, but your old sinful nature remains just beneath the surface.
⊕ An ongoing tension rages between the two natures.
⊕ Do not underestimate the power of the old nature or the limits of its depravity.
⊕ The nature you nourish will have the greatest influence in your life.

# Moral Minefields

*"So I strive always to keep my conscience clear before God and man" (Acts 24:16).*

IS IT POSSIBLE TO LIVE A PURE, GODLY LIFE in the military? Can you participate in all of the military's activities and maintain a clear conscience before God and man? Aren't there *more* temptations in the military? Isn't there more peer pressure to join in others' immoral activity? Will you go in singing God's praise and come out "swearing like a sailor"?

If you are a Christian who ever considered military service, these questions likely went through your mind. There is some truth to the negative stereotypes that depict military life. History is full of stories of drunken sailors, soldiers, and more recently, airmen. Military men are infamous for having a "girl in every port." These vices associated with the military are not limited to the lower enlisted grades. In recent years, senior NCOs and officers have been prosecuted for using their position to obtain sexual favors from subordinates.

So, *can* a Christian serve in the military and live a consistently obedient and pure life? This is an important question. You should understand the environment you enter when you join the military. You must learn to differentiate between fitting in with your peers and giving in to negative peer pressure. Be on the lookout for moral "minefields" and understand the consequences of walking through them.

A minefield is a good way to think of hidden moral dangers. A minefield is a piece of ground sown with hidden explosives. They are difficult to detect—on the surface there appears to be no danger—but are almost always deadly. Only a fool would enter a known minefield.

*A prudent man sees danger and takes refuge, but the simple keep going and suffer for it (Proverbs 22:3).*

If you had a battlefield map marked with minefields, you would not walk through the dangerous areas. Not wanting to be maimed or killed, you would pay attention to the dangers and avoid them. Moral minefields are the same. Certain activities and practices will damage your life and your soul. But God has provided you with a map, the Bible, that clearly identifies the dangerous traps you will face. The consequences of falling into these traps are equally clear.

*But a man who commits adultery lacks judgment; whoever does so destroys himself (Proverbs 6:32).*

*"For that would have been shameful, a sin to be judged. It is a fire that burns to Destruction; it would have uprooted my harvest" (Job 31:11–12).*

*Dear friends, I urge you, as aliens and strangers in the world, to abstain from sinful desires, which war against your soul (1 Peter 2:11).*

This is just a sample of the verses that warn of the danger and describe the results of sinful behavior. Notice something important: These verses don't talk about future judgment for sin, but the *present* destruction of the soul. There will be a future judgment for offenses against God and man, but the emphasis here is the self-inflicted torment for the person who abandons God's way for a life of rebellion. During your life, you will encounter moral minefields. They will injure, even kill, those who ignore the warnings. The good news is that they *are* well marked.

## COMMON MINEFIELDS

Moral minefields do not exist only in the military. The writer of 1 Corinthians said, "No temptation has seized you except what is common to man" (1 Corinthians 10:13a). People face dangerous temptations in most occupations. The circumstances and rationalizations may have a different twist, but the results are the same.

Here are some of the "mines" that invite participation and reward the curious and foolish with personal devastation.

### *Sexual impurity*

God speaks clearly about the issue of sex. Sex was created by God and was given to us as His good gift to be enjoyed within the boundaries of His will. However, like electricity, gasoline, and atomic energy, sex is a powerful force. Within the appropriate "container," all of these powerful energies are good and useful. Outside of the container, they are dangerous, volatile, and harmful. Consider these strong warnings from God:

> But among you there must not be even a hint of sexual immorality, or of any kind of impurity, or of greed, because these are improper for God's holy people. Nor should there be obscenity, foolish talk or coarse joking, which are out of place, but rather thanksgiving. For of this you can be sure: No immoral, impure or greedy person—

*such a man is an idolater—has any inheritance in the kingdom of Christ and of God (Ephesians 5:3–5).*

*It is God's will that you should be sanctified: that you should avoid sexual immorality; that each of you should learn to control his own body in a way that is holy and honorable, not in passionate lust like the heathen, who do not know God (1 Thessalonians 4:3–5).*

Sexual purity is a primary concern to God. He created us male and female. He established the "container"—marriage—for sexual activity. He understands the high price of disobedience in this area. Sexual purity is maintained by focusing *all* of your sexual attraction and energy on your husband or wife, and no other! Monogamous commitment can be violated in numerous ways. These include marital infidelity (adultery), promiscuous activity by those who are unmarried (fornication), and affairs of the mind (pornography).

Chapter 15 emphasized the importance of fellowship for mutual encouragement and protection. The struggle to be sexually pure is more manageable when a group of men or women commit themselves to support and hold one another accountable. If this is a battle for you, do not fight it alone.

### Abuse of legal and illegal drugs

Marijuana, cocaine, amphetamines, barbiturates, and alcohol have dashed many military careers. The first four drugs are illegal and banned for anyone in the military. The last one is also a drug, although many people don't think of beer, wine, and liquor this way. But, like other drugs, alcohol suppresses brain activity and dangerously alters judgment and behavior. With a certain level of alcohol in the blood, some activities become illegal, such as driving a car, flying a plane, or reporting for duty. Alcohol is a powerful, dangerous drug. You must decide for yourself whether or not you will drink at all. If you choose to drink, establish firm limits before you start. The risks, potential danger, social pressure, and cost all need to be evaluated in the "light of day." Views on drinking have varied with the tides of history and societal whim. Ultimately, you need to find out from your Creator, not your peers, what is right for you.

> *Who has woe? Who has sorrow? Who has strife? Who has complaints? Who has needless bruises? Who has blood-shot eyes? Those who linger over wine, who go to sample bowls of mixed wine. Do not gaze at wine when it is red, when it sparkles in the cup, when it goes down smoothly! In the end it bites like a snake and poisons like a viper. Your eyes will see strange sights and your mind imagine confus-ing things. You will be like one sleeping on the high seas, lying on top of the rigging. "They hit me," you will say, "but I'm not hurt! They beat me, but I don't feel it! When will I wake up so I can find another drink?" (Proverbs 23:29–35).*

### Impure speech

It is easy to pick up impure, blasphemous speech when you're surrounded by it. But God establishes a high standard for our speech. To choose to follow God's command in this area will assuredly identify you as "different." One soldier committed to pure speech can profoundly impact a whole duty section. Others are often spurred to better language by only one or two good examples. This is another area in which fellowship and encour-agement from other Christians can help. It's not easy to control your language, but once you make the commitment to try, you'll find that it soon becomes natural.

General George Washington addressed this topic with his soldiers in the 18th century:

"The General is sorry to be informed that the foolish and wicked practice of profane cursing and swearing, a vice heretofore little known in an American army, is growing into fashion. He hopes the officers will, by example as well as influence, endeavor to check it, and that both they and the men will reflect, that we can have little hope of the blessing of Heaven on our arms, if we insult it by our impiety and folly. Added to that it is a vice so mean and low, without any temptation, that every man of sense and character detests and despises it" (a General Order issued August 3, 1776 by General George Washington).

The apostle Paul also spoke on this subject:

*Do not let any unwholesome talk come out of your mouths, but only what is helpful for building others up according to their needs, that it may benefit those who listen (Ephesians 4:29).*

## Lying

We've already looked at honesty (Chapter 13), so to mention it again might seem redundant. But integrity is of highest importance in the military. In fact, military service demands it. Lying is inconsistent with the trust invested in the keepers of the national defense. However, there are pressures that can lead even the most honest men and women into deception.

The military values success, perhaps more than any other organization, because to be second in warfare is to lose. Preparation for war is measured in readiness. Units and individuals are expected to be ready and provide regular "readiness" reports. The pressure to give a positive report can be intense. If other units are reporting "fully ready" and your unit is not, the pressure increases. The pressure to look good can challenge warriors to report falsely high levels of readiness. This is a familiar example, and it always leads to the detriment of the unit.

Imagine the gas gauge in your car reporting what it knows you want to see! It knows you will be unhappy with an empty tank, so it chooses to shade the information, reporting that the gas tank is just a little bit more full than it is. You would be furious if you found out your sneaky gas gauge had fed you this slightly improved view of reality, especially when you ran out of gas.

False reporting has been a temptation for so many years, it has its own name. It is referred to as "CYA," which translates "Cover Your A _ _" (the "A" word referring to the lower backside of your anatomy). The pressure to show the right numbers affects individuals at all levels. They get caught up in "padding" number of hours flown, number of rounds fired, number of meals served. The scenario usually follows this pattern:

➤ A goal is established.
➤ Individuals/units are required to report their results in reaching the goal.
➤ They realize that the goal will not be reached (often for good reasons).
➤ They file a false report stating that the goal was achieved.

Every warrior should detest false reporting. It is shortsighted and dangerous. As a Christian, bound by commitment to God, you will be additionally challenged if you find yourself in a situation in which false reporting is encouraged or required. Be prepared to choose integrity and truth at all costs.

*Kings take pleasure in honest lips; they value a man who speaks the truth (Proverbs 16:13).*

## CHOOSING TO LIVE RIGHT

On first reading, you may think to yourself, "These things are clearly wrong." You would not willingly become involved in any of these destructive practices. You are, after all, a Christian. So why is this chapter even in the book?

In the light of day, with the warnings of Scripture fixed clearly in your mind, the temptations seem weak, unreasonable, and easy to avoid. But life is not always lived in places of light and clarity. Many paths with pleasant, enticing beginnings lead to destruction. A "golden opportunity" may be nothing more than the gate to a moral minefield. There are several "keys" that open these deceptive gates, allowing you to stroll mindlessly into the minefields. You will recognize them; you have heard most of them before:

➤ "Everyone else is doing it."
➤ "No one will ever know." (The military variant to this one is "What goes on TDY, stays on TDY." TDY means temporary duty at a site away from home base. In other words, as long as you are not around the people who know you, you can do whatever you want without it getting back to them.)
➤ "It will just be this one time."
➤ "You've got to live a little."
➤ "Try it, you don't know what you're missing."
➤ "It's really not that bad."

Many of these phrases use a minimizing modifier, such as "just" or "only." Do not let yourself minimize your actions or their consequences. If something is "not that bad," it may be *really awful.* "Just this one time" may lead you down a long, tragic road.

Living your life according to God's values will cause you to be different. Maybe others in your unit want to live lives of integrity, too. That will make it easier for all of you. If you find that you are

174

the only one embracing biblical values, the commitment to live an upright life will be more difficult. Christian warriors need to develop moral and mental toughness to choose absolute obedience to God, regardless of the number of others who choose that path. Consider these words, spoken by three young men who were about to be punished for choosing to do the right thing:

> *Shadrach, Meshach and Abednego replied to the king, "O Nebuchadnezzar, we do not need to defend ourselves before you in this matter. If we are thrown into the blazing furnace, the God we serve is able to save us from it, and he will rescue us from your hand, O king. But even if he does not, we want you to know, O king, that we will not serve your gods or worship the image of gold you have set up" (Daniel 3:16–18).*

*"Even if He does not."* They chose the right path, whether it worked in their favor or not. This is the way you must approach the moral minefields you face if you are going to be "light" to the people around you. These are tough decisions. Be encouraged that many have made them before and have completed honorable and successful military careers. You can, too.

 **SUMMARY**

- ⊕ Some dangerous, immoral practices are associated with military life.
- ⊕ You must learn to differentiate between fitting in with your peers and giving in to peer pressure.
- ⊕ Rationalizing harmful behavior falsely diminishes individual responsibility and the possible consequences.
- ⊕ Every person must give account to God for his or her choices. Choose absolute obedience to Him.

# Individuality and Conformity

*For you created my inmost being; you knit me together in my mother's womb. I praise you because I am fearfully and wonderfully made; your works are wonderful, I know that full well. My frame was not hidden from you when I was made in the secret place. When I was woven together in the depths of the earth, your eyes saw my unformed body. All the days ordained for me were written in your book before one of them came to be. How precious to me are your thoughts, O God! How vast is the sum of them! Were I to count them, they would outnumber the grains of sand. When I awake, I am still with you (Psalm 139:13–18).*

THIS VERSE AFFIRMS THE UNIQUENESS of every created being. Each individual is different from others. Even identical twins with exactly the same genes have different personalities and interests. Stop and think about this amazing fact. From the beginning of our days, even in the womb, we were specially designed and shaped. The fact that every new human being is an entirely different creature from any previous one makes the world interesting.

Think for a minute what your hometown would be like if every person were an exact copy of you! Think of the variety of personalities and talents that would be unrepresented. We should thank God continually, not only for our individuality, but also for our differences.

## INDIVIDUALITY IN THE MILITARY

Because individuality is a prominent feature of humanity, what happens when you are subjected to the pressures of systematic uniformity? Do you lose your uniqueness? Can you be true to your own distinct character and to the military's expectations at the same time?

Webster's Dictionary defines "conformity" as *"to cause to be of the same form."* The military has a clear agenda: Warriors must conform to its required regulations, standards, and traditions to achieve some measure of uniformity. This causes a tension between maintaining your individuality and conforming to the organization. The tension is resolved by finding balance between these opposites. Achieving this balance is relatively simple if you apply wisdom to your circumstances and employ the best parts of each.

In the military, you will find areas in which you clearly need to make every effort to conform. At other times, your unit will be best served when you exercise your individuality. But how do you know when to seek conformity and when to express your individuality? This challenge is not unique to the military. Read through the 12th chapter of 1 Corinthians, which discusses the same tension in the church. God ordained each person to be different, yet He commanded unity to flow from diversity.

*But in fact God has arranged the parts in the body, every one of them, just as he wanted them to be. If they were all one part, where would the body be? As it is, there are many parts, but one body (1 Corinthians 12:18–20, emphasis added).*

The best ways to sort out this challenge is to spend time thinking through the issue ahead of time. List in three blocks areas in which you need to conform, to use your individuality, or to resist conformity. The spectrum of conformity in the military ranges from high expectations to low or no expectations. It looks something like this:

| Level of Conformity | Example |
| --- | --- |
| High (conformity is necessary) | Life-and-death situations |
| | Appearance |
| | Military procedures |
| | Preparation/use of weapons |
| | Flight operations |
| Medium (a mix of conformity and individuality) | Completion rate of training courses |
| | Written and oral reports |
| | Individual physical training |
| | Maintenance procedures |
| Low (mostly individual choice) | What to eat |
| | Use of personal time |
| | Hobbies |
| | Religious practices |
| | Political party |

There's no question about it. Conformity is part of being in the military, and for good reason. When soldiers are armed, it is imperative that no one fires a weapon until given the command. Similarly, when the "cease-fire" command is given, everyone must stop. When the command "forward march" is given, everyone must step off with the same foot at the same time. Weapon maintenance must be done in a step-by-step way, without deviation or variation. There is no margin for personal choice in these situations.

Other tasks, however, encourage trouble-shooting and individual initiative. In a job like weather forecasting, the technician studies the data, but the forecast is based on logic and human analysis. The less exact and critical the task, the more individual thinking is allowed and encouraged. For example, each military person wears his or her uniform a little differently, even though it may not be obvious. Soldiers have their own ways to eliminate dangling threads and keep pocket flaps down, their own secrets for keeping shirts tucked in and socks up. It's ironic that the military "uniform" has so many variations.

In still other areas, such as religious choice and political party, the military has no expectation of conformity. Hobbies and free-time activities are other examples, although your options may be temporarily limited aboard a submarine or in a war zone.

## THE VALUE OF INDIVIDUAL THINKING

The military encourages and benefits from creative suggestions submitted through proper channels. For example, a maintenance task may require seven steps and an expenditure of $6,000 worth of parts. After completing the task several times, a technician may discover a way it could be done better in five steps with only $3,000 worth of parts. The military encourages individuals to be alert for new and improved techniques and to request changes through formal channels (such as using the suggestion program and technical manual revision processes).

Imagine an extreme survival situation. A four-person special-forces platoon is stranded in the wilderness. Outwardly, the four appear very much alike. They are wearing the same uniform and have much of the same training. But one is better at catching small animals with snares and begins to lay out traps to gather food. Another is experienced with signals and begins to gather wood and green leaves to make a smoke signal. Each one contributes individual skill and expertise. In even the smallest and most uniform group, there is healthy variation that benefits the whole group.

## WHEN CONFORMITY IS BAD

As in all walks of life, there are pressures in the military to conform to destructive, immoral activities. Chapter 17 talked about some of these; here's another: Many young people turn 21 while in the military. Because the soldier can now legally drink, the expectation is that he should go out drinking on his 21st birthday. Is this a reasonable expectation? Must you conform to it?

Consider another example. To sound cool and be part of the group, you may feel pressure to talk like the rest of the group, including using profanity. Think about this. Is it a reasonable expectation? Who imposes it? What sort of penalty would you face if you didn't conform? These are questions you need to think through as you consider issues at the low end of the conformity spectrum. Certain values in society will shape your thinking and actions. Be aware of these and resist conforming to values and practices that are not honoring to God.

The J. B. Phillips translation of Romans 12:2 says, "Don't let the world around you squeeze you into its own mould." The world will try to push and squeeze you into its mold of expectations. In the process of trying to wiggle and bend into that shape, you run the risk of losing your unique creativity and spontaneity. God, on the other hand, wants to transform you into His image, an altogether more beneficial process.

## FIND THE BALANCE

The military demands a high level of conformity from its members in many duty-related areas. This is necessary when the actions of many individuals and many units must be coordinated. Yet even in the military, there is room for creativity and originality. God made you a unique individual, and your individual thoughts and talents will benefit your unit and your country.

Balance will come in proportion to your maturity and wisdom. Even in areas that demand absolute conformity, your individuality allows, even encourages, innovation and improvement, if channeled appropriately.

## SUMMARY

⊕ God designed each of us as unique individuals.

⊕ For good reasons, the military requires a high level of conformity.

⊕ Although individuals are all unique, much can be accomplished in groups where conformity to standard practices benefits everyone.

⊕ In the military, creativity and innovation are highly valued if channeled appropriately.

⊕ Increasing wisdom and maturity will help you determine when and where to conform.

## CHAPTER 19

# Time Management

*"Show me, O LORD, my life's end and the number of my days; let me know how fleeting is my life. You have made my days a mere handbreadth; the span of my years is as nothing before you. Each man's life is but a breath"* (Psalm 39:4–5).

IN THE MILITARY, YOUR TIME is not your own. You serve under leaders who have authority to control much of your day. Most of your time will be used fulfilling the requirements of your military unit. Twelve-hour shifts are common. During times of increased readiness and in combat situations, you can expect even longer shifts. Military service makes extensive demands on an individual's time. While everyone gets 24 hours in a day, if you're in the military, your amount of discretionary time may be severely limited.

### WHAT FREE TIME?
The military will keep you busy. Chapter 4 of this book described the elements of military work. Chapter 7 discussed the supplemental requirements of professional development. In addition to these, you have daily requirements to prepare uniforms and equipment. Training, testing, and recurring certification are heaped on your already busy schedule. You'll also have additional duties that support the whole organization:

guard duty, food preparation and distribution, duty desk/orderly, and so on. Finally, you've got to make time for the basics—eating, exercise, and sleep—so you can maintain fighting condition.

Yet, even in the most intense and demanding environments, you will have some personal time. Throughout history, soldiers have found a few minutes to write letters, wash laundry, and accomplish other small but important tasks. In a peacetime environment, you will generally have free weekends and holidays. You'll also have opportunities to take leave from your unit occasionally. In these circumstances, you will find yourself in the unfamiliar position of having complete control over your time.

## SCHEDULING YOUR TIME

The key to using time effectively over the long haul is deliberate planning, scheduling, and habit building. In the military, you can't plan in isolation because of the many demands on your time. Scheduling "your" time is like painting a picture with three artists. The first artist steps up to the canvas and roughly outlines what the picture will look like. The next artist adds color and shading. The final artist fills in detail, bringing the picture to life.

In the "painting" of your life, the military's requirements fill in most of your day's events, including wake-up time, grooming, dressing, duty hours, and meal times. Your unit and supervisor provide the next level of detail, including specific job tasks, your training schedule, and duty rosters. But *you* are always the final artist. It is your right and responsibility to add the details. You decide how to use your discretionary time and even how you will use your time at work and in training. Your life and efforts will resemble the rest of your unit except for the decisions you make as the "third artist."

The fundamental principle of time management is this: Use *all* of it well. Don't waste any of it. Now let's look at some of the ways you can use time: spend, invest, save, and waste.

### Spend

Time is spent when minutes are used to produce something. The time could be used to repair a radio, read a technical manual, conduct a training session, serve guard duty, or fly a mission. "Spending" is the most common way we use time. It is an even exchange of something useful done for time spent, usually resulting in a sense of fulfillment. Time is closely related to money. When you spend money and get something of equal value in return, you are pleased. If you spend your money or your time and have little to show for it, you feel a sense of loss. Even this sense of loss can be useful if you learn how to use your time more wisely in the future.

### Invest

Investing time is similar to investing money: a portion of your time is used with an eye toward the future. You expect a greater return on an "investment" than on time simply "spent." Most exercise and conditioning fall in the category of investment. The time used is exchanged for increased physical stamina and endurance.

A soldier may accomplish a familiar task several times in an hour. Once the task is learned, the exchange of time for production is simply spending. For example, a soldier knows how to disassemble, clean, and reassemble his rifle. He can do this task well because he has done it so many times. Then he decides he should learn how to do this in the dark in case he someday needs to repair his weapon without the advantage of light. As he trains himself in the new skill, he transitions from *spending* time to *investing* it as he learns a skill that may be useful in the future.

In this example, it's easy to see the difference between *spending* and *investing* time. It's not always so simple. Much of the time you spend training and doing your job is also an investment in the future. Making the distinction, however, is a worthwhile exercise. At the end of each day, ask yourself, "Did I use my time wisely today? Did I merely spend it all, or did I invest some of it with an eye toward the future?"

Most people *spend* nearly all of their time. Deliberately plan to *invest* some of your hours improving your ability, understanding, and strengths.

You can also invest your time by using it on others. The classic example of this is a teacher, who uses time to help others. People who repeatedly teach courses or skills are not looking for improvement in their own ability, but they expect a huge dividend in the capability and output of those they teach. They are investing in others.

Chapters 9 and 10 of this book described ways to invest time in helping people grow spiritually. Jesus invested His life in His disciples so they were able to carry on His ministry after He was gone. Paul invested in the life of Timothy and others. You also have the ability to invest in people's lives. This means using portions of your day that you would normally spend on yourself to help, encourage, and teach others. Your investment pays off when you see others growing in character and spiritual maturity.

> *"The man who had received the five talents went at once and put his money to work and gained five more"* *(Matthew 25:16).*

### Save

We have compared money to time throughout this chapter, but here's where the comparison ends. Saving time is not the same as saving money. Money can be put aside and used later; that is not true of time. In what way, then, can time be saved? If you are more effective in completing a task, you can finish it sooner, giving yourself additional time to do something else. Most electrical appliances are advertised as "time-saving" devices, which they are. Time saving is a two-part equation, though. If a machine is used to save time, the remaining "saved time" must be either spent or invested. If the time saved is wasted, then any time saved was really lost. This is not uncommon in our modern world. We have many devices that save us time—washing machines, dishwashers, and microwave ovens to name just a few—but what do we do with all the time we're saving? Often, we waste it. To really matter, any time we save must be used effectively.

Another way to save time is to double use it, otherwise known as multitasking. Some military jobs require your presence but little mental or physical energy. If you serve at a duty desk on a graveyard shift, it's not hard to double use your time. You're getting credit for serving a shift on duty, but you can often spend much of the time reading or studying. One task requires your physical presence and the other uses your mind.

The on-duty fireman provides another good example of double using time. While alert for a call, the fireman cleans and maintains the truck, practices life-saving techniques, and even sleeps. Many daily activities lend themselves to double use. What does your mind do while you're showering every morning? What about while you're running to stay in shape? Or while you're standing for long periods in formation, or waiting for transportation? Everyone has significant blocks of time that could be double used, thus saving time in the future for other activities.

*Be very careful, then, how you live—not as unwise but as wise, making the most of every opportunity, because the days are evil (Ephesians 5:15–16).*

### *Waste*

It is easy to waste time; you simply need to do nothing. Certainly every minute of every day does not need to be crammed with activity. (We'll talk about the need for relaxation and recreation later.) However, there are an unlimited number of activities that invite us to "kick back" or "take it easy." Here is a partial list of big time-wasters. You may have others on your own list.

➤ **Television.** Most people watch too much television and recall little or nothing of what they have seen. Some watch back-to-back sports events. By the time the third or fourth game is over, they cannot recall the score of the first—or even who played! Much has been written on the ills of television. One of the great tragedies is that, in the name of education, countless hours are squandered watching TV instead of actually learning something. Not only that, but television watching develops passivity and suppresses physiological processes.

➤ **Video games.** This modern phenomenon is linked to the proliferation of computers. Video games used to be played in arcades, and play was limited by the number of quarters in your pocket. Not anymore. Games can be played any time, anywhere, sending hours of valuable time down the drain. Never has so much time been wasted by so many with so little to show for it. What about games that claim to provide "virtual reality"? That phrase should offend us. If your reality is *virtual,* it's not reality!

➤ **Phones, Internet, and e-mail.** Instant communication and information are at your fingertips, causing people to spend increasing time on phones and computers. Where phones used to reach only as far as their cords allowed, now they go almost everywhere—automobiles, stores, parks, and gyms. Cell phones allow for little or no control over incoming calls, causing their owners to be interrupted anywhere during any activity. Technology in the form of "Web surfing" has also become a major consumer of discretionary time. Each of these communication tools can be of great use if used wisely but a great waste of time if not.

➤ **Sports.** This potentially good activity has lost a lot of its goodness. If people *participated* in one hour of physical activity for every hour of sports watched, we would be a much healthier society. Sports activities are intended to condition the body and push it to higher levels of health and endurance, but most sports today are spectator sports. Professionals play the sport, while thousands sit and watch. Wonderful conditioning sports such as tennis, track, basketball, and soccer have become opportunities to generate excitement and revenue, while our personal hemoglobin thins and our cholesterol thickens.

➤ **"Hangin' around."** This nonactivity has many aliases: "cruising," "chilling," and "killing time." Its participants pour countless hours of time into a cesspool of planned idleness. It not only allows, but also encourages mental passivity.

## RELAXATION AND RECREATION
Everyone needs a chance to restore their bodies, minds, emotions, and energy. Relaxation is a legitimate, God-constructed need. Every day, your body needs to sleep. While you're asleep, your body is able to restore tissues, recharge your energy, and prepare for the next waking period.

Your mind and soul also need periods of rest, and this is where recreation comes in. In modern times, we have established a five-day workweek, setting aside two days at the end of the week for other activities. Much of these two days should be used for recreation. (This should be pronounced "re-creation" rather than "wreck-reation"—a time when your mind and soul are renewed and restored, not wrecked!) God required the Jews to rest on the Sabbath. No such law exists in the New Testament, but the necessity for rest flows from the way we are created. We need rest and recuperation. The military has figured that out. Soldiers exposed to high intensity combat conditions are eventually assigned to "R&R" (rest and recuperation) locations. This time off makes the soldiers more effective in the long run.

God designed people to:
➤ Worship God
➤ Work at a job
➤ Play at recreation

Most people today have missed this plan. Instead, they:
➤ Worship their work
➤ Work at recreation
➤ Play at worship

When we worship our work, we don't allow sufficient time for recreation and worship of God. This is a question of priority. What is really first in your life? Periodically evaluate your use of time. What does it say about the way you prioritize your relationship with God, your use of free time, and the relative importance you place on time at work?

## DELIBERATE PLANNING

One who fails to plan, plans to fail. Time moves along without any encouragement from us. It's a resource that can be squandered or maximized. To use time most effectively, its use must be planned. The surfer understands this concept. He floats on top of his board, looking out to sea. He looks for the rising swell that will turn into a wave as it reaches him. He prepares for the arrival of the wave by turning his board toward shore; then he paddles to pick up speed. When the wave arrives, if he has done everything correctly, he simply mounts the board and rides the wave toward the beach.

At the beginning of each week, you can see a week's worth of hours hurling toward you. If you prepare in advance, you can make the most of the inevitable wave of time that will come and go. To do this, think through how you will use your daily minutes and hours. Make a list of all that needs to be done and put the list in priority order. Be sure to include things like work, sleep, meals, and even free time, which you might use to take a nap or go for a run. Your schedule will take shape around the most important activities. Some things will have to be cut for lack of time. The goal is not to fill up your schedule with activity; it's to wisely use the "wave" headed your way.

At the end of the week, look back over the schedule. What was completed as scheduled, and what did not get done? Adapt the next week's schedule to make it more workable. People who plan their activities usually do not schedule blocks for "wasting time" or "mindless hours of TV watching." Deliberate preplanning will eliminate most wasted time.

This kind of methodical planning and scheduling comes naturally for some people, but is much harder for others. Regardless of your personality type, you need to do *some* planning and scheduling. If this is a stretch for you, find someone who enjoys it who can help you.

*Let the wise listen and add to their learning, and let the discerning get guidance (Proverbs 1:5).*

### MAKE THE MOST OF YOUR TIME

The military makes heavy demands on its soldiers, sailors, and airmen. During periods of increased readiness and combat, your time will be totally dedicated to serving the military. At other periods, you will have more control over how you spend your time. Think ahead and plan how you will use this time. Will you spend, invest, save, or waste it?

*The plans of the diligent lead to profit (Proverbs 21:5a).*

## SUMMARY

⊕ The military makes huge demands on your time.

⊕ You are still responsible for how you use your time on and off duty.

⊕ Make an effort to save and invest your time instead of just spending or wasting it.

⊕ A little prior planning goes a long way in making the most of your time.

⊕ Time is a gift from God. Be a good steward of it.

# Principles of War

*Then the dragon was enraged at the woman and went off to make war against the rest of her offspring—those who obey God's commandments and hold to the testimony of Jesus (Revelation 12:17).*

*Put on the full armor of God so that you can take your stand against the devil's schemes. For our struggle is not against flesh and blood, but against the rulers, against the authorities, against the powers of this dark world and against the spiritual forces of evil in the heavenly realms (Ephesians 6:11–12).*

THE SPIRITUAL WAR THAT RAGES EVERY DAY—mostly unseen by human eyes—is the most significant battle you will ever be involved in. The consequences are the most important you will ever know. The precious, eternal lives of all men and women are at stake in this war between light and darkness. Satan's objective is to destroy lives through the ravages of sin and lead them away from God for all eternity. God, on the other hand, wants to lead people into a fulfilling life on earth and prepare them for eternal life in His presence. When the objectives are stated this clearly, you may wonder why there is a war at all. Why would anybody side with Satan?

Satan is a liar and a deceiver, and humans, on their own,

do not see through his deception. He promises one thing and delivers another. He poses as an angel of light but enslaves people in darkness. He attacks when we are tired and alone. He can and will defeat those who are not protected by the armor of God.

Every Christian is a soldier in the army of God, even civilians who have no real combat experience. People who are soldiers in this life have an advantage over their civilian Christian brothers and sisters. As a Christian who is also a soldier, you spend your days focused on defense, offense, and victory. When the Bible discusses warfare and weapons, you have the knowledge and experience that help you understand these word pictures. You can relate the principles of warfare you have been taught in the military to the war you wage as a Christian.

## TIME-TESTED PRINCIPLES

Over a period of several hundred years, the Principles of War have been distilled, defined, refined, and committed to paper by people who have studied the art and science of war. These are broad principles that govern success or failure in warfare. From these principles come doctrine, strategy, and tactics. Nearly every military person will receive some instruction on these principles during their career.

The Principles of War are often used as a guide to review plans. Does the plan consider the major principles that govern war? Has the plan overlooked some important aspect that might result in defeat? The plan is held up to "the light" of time-proven principles to check for gaps or weaknesses.

This chapter examines spiritual warfare in light of the Principles of War. We'll define each principle, find its biblical counterpart in Scripture, and discuss some practical applications. You can use this chapter periodically as an evaluation tool, individually or with a group of other believers. Weigh your own beliefs, behavior, and plans against these principles and see if you're using them to experience the victorious life God has for you.

*But thanks be to God! He gives us the victory through our Lord Jesus Christ (1 Corinthians 15:57).*

After you've evaluated these principles in a spiritual context, focus on the leader, Jesus Christ, and prepare for war using the assets and armor He provides.

*Therefore put on the full armor of God, so that when the day of evil comes, you may be able to stand your ground, and after you have done everything, to stand (Ephesians 6:13).*

## THE PRINCIPLES

**Objective** (Purpose)—The foundation upon which all warfare should rest is a clear and concise statement of what is to be achieved. There should be a central goal or purpose to which all other goals and actions contribute. A clear *objective* protects the soldier from losing focus and wasting energy and resources in activities that do not contribute to victory.

*But* one thing I do: *Forgetting what is behind and straining toward what is ahead, I press on toward the goal to win the prize for which God has called me heavenward in Christ Jesus (Philippians 3:13b–14, emphasis added).*

Our *objective,* as Christians, is to love and obey God with all of our heart, soul, mind, and strength. We are to be Christ's disciples and make new disciples as we go about the business of life. Regardless of how active we are or how tired we are at the end of the day, if our actions and words do not contribute to this *objective,* we are not winning.

Keep your purpose clearly in focus. Ask yourself occasionally, "Is everything I'm doing contributing to my *objective?*" Be tough with yourself. Purposefully focus on doing the things that contribute to your relationship with God and obedience to His commands. Let others help evaluate your activities. Learn to challenge and encourage one another to be focused and productive.

*And let us consider how we may spur one another on toward love and good deeds (Hebrews 10:24).*

**Initiative** (Offensive)—The principle of *initiative* is to act rather than react, and it flows from the *objective*. Taking the offensive allows the commander to choose the place, time, and method of warfare. *Initiative* keeps the enemy off-guard and in retreat. Failure to take the offensive results in always being on the defense.

*For God did not give us a spirit of timidity, but a spirit of power, of love and of self-discipline. So do not be ashamed to testify about our Lord, or ashamed of me his prisoner. But join with me in suffering for the gospel, by the power of God (2 Timothy 1:7–8).*

Christians need to be on the offensive. The Christian life should be full of power and boldness because the outcome is already known. Yet too many Christians adopt the philosophy of "Speak only when spoken to." All evil needs in order to triumph is for God's people to say nothing. If we wait for something to happen, we will continually be on the defense.

Your offensive begins with time alone in prayer as you seek God's power, boldness, and control in all circumstances. Ask Him to prepare the hearts and minds of people you will speak to today. Ask Him to give you a "hearing" with people who don't know the Gospel and who need true joy in their lives. Then, take action! Take and make opportunities to speak. Speak up, in love, against sinful practices. Help people compare their beliefs to the eternal Word of God.

The armor of God, listed in Ephesians 6, mentions only one weapon for offense: the sword of the Spirit, which is the Word of God. The other pieces of equipment are all defensive. Know the Word of God well enough to use it in all of life's circumstances.

Christianity is not a position; it is a movement! It is not a philosophy; it is a life-gripping reality! Through your words and your actions, take *initiative* that will help you achieve your *objective*.

*Dear children, let us not love with words or tongue but with actions and in truth (1 John 3:18).*

**Mobility** (Maneuver, Movement)—*Mobility* is action that places one's strength against the enemy's weakness. To maneuver is to avoid engaging the enemy at a strong point. It involves a willingness to see, adjust, innovate, and keep moving. *Mobility* allows an army to strike while strong, then disengage and reinforce, and then strike again. *Mobility* demands a careful understanding of battlefield conditions and a willingness to move for advantage.

*Therefore, prepare your minds for action; be self-controlled; set your hope fully on the grace to be given you when Jesus Christ is revealed (1 Peter 1:13).*

The principle of *mobility* flows from *initiative*. For Christians to maintain the *initiative,* they need to be flexible and innovative. Christians through the ages have discovered ways and words to communicate the hope of the Gospel to their generation.

Today, we have the benefit of modern technology to reach the lost world with the Gospel. We can send taped messages or music to friends. E-mail gives us the ability to communicate with almost any other person, anywhere in the world. This is ultimate *mobility* for sharing the Gospel.

We also need to be good listeners. The message of the Gospel should be shaped in response to people's needs. Jesus was a master at this. He listened, then spoke to people's point of need. He delivered the strength of God's Word at a point of need and sensitivity. Our words and actions should follow this approach. Have a clear understanding of the unchanging Gospel, and present the strength of God's Word at people's points of weakness and need. This is a skill that develops as you listen carefully to what people are saying and feel what they are feeling.

The closeness you experience in military living and working conditions allows greater intimacy and understanding of those around you. When you live in a communal facility, you have greater access and opportunity to observe, listen, and share appropriately with others. The same is true if you're aboard a ship or among a crew assigned to a common task (such as flying an airplane or firing an artillery piece). Regardless of your circumstance, be alert and look for opportunities to use your *mobility* to pursue your *objective.*

**Flexibility** (Freedom of Action)—*Flexibility* supports the principle of *mobility,* allowing for positive change in response to unexpected circumstance, adversity, or unforeseen enemy action. *Flexibility* allows the commander to respond appropriately to change and opposition, while still maintaining the *offensive.*

*To the Jews I became like a Jew, to win the Jews. To those under the law I became like one under the law (though I myself am not under the law), so as to win those under the law. To those not having the law I became like one not having the law (though I am not free from God's law but am under Christ's law), so as to win those not having the law. To the weak I became weak, to win the weak. I have become all things to all men so that by all possible means I might save some (1 Corinthians 9:20–22, emphasis added).*

Life in the military is full of change—locations, duty schedules, and work assignments can change daily. It's also unpredictable. Your transport to a maneuver location may arrive late or not at all. A supporting unit may be unable to assist in a planned task, so plans for the day must change. The Air Force has coined this well-worn phrase: "Flexibility is the key to airpower."

*Flexibility* is also the key to living successfully as a Christian. As you plan your day, realize that there may be changes, and trust in a loving and caring God who places you in whatever circumstances will allow you to serve Him best. Don't be frustrated by blocked opportunities. Instead, look for a better time or way to accomplish what you had planned. With head up and eyes open, face each event as God-ordained, looking for opportunities to act and speak as Jesus would.

*Now listen, you who say, "Today or tomorrow we will go to this or that city, spend a year there, carry on business and make money." Why, you do not even know what will happen tomorrow. What is your life? You are a mist that appears for a little while and then vanishes. Instead, you ought to say, "If it is the Lord's will, we will live and do this or that" (James 4:13–15).*

**Unity of Command**—This principle suggests that appropriate authority and responsibility be assigned to a single commander to bring unity to an assignment. It unites all forces in pursuit of a common goal.

*There is one body and one Spirit—just as you were called to one hope when you were called—one Lord, one faith, one baptism; one God and Father of all, who is over all and through all and in all (Ephesians 4:4–6).*

All Christians have one "Commander"—Jesus Christ. He is the one who gives direction to our lives. When Christians align their behavior, attitudes, and speech with Jesus' commands, the body of believers is unified.

Jesus said the one who obeyed Him was the one who loved Him and was His disciple (John 14:21). Examine your motives and actions to be sure you are not trying to usurp or undercut Jesus' rightful authority over your life. He must lead, and you must follow. Pattern your leadership after His—serving, ministering, sacrificing. Align your every thought, word, and deed with the pattern of Jesus' life and commands.

**Cohesion** (Cooperation, Communication)—*Cohesion* is the immeasurable but very real force that holds the various elements of combat forces together in battle. *Cohesion* flows from a single *objective* and *unity of command*. It comes from each combatant understanding and being committed to the plan and making every effort to coordinate his or her efforts with allied forces.

*My brothers, some . . . have informed me that there are quarrels among you. What I mean is this: One of you says, "I follow Paul"; another, "I follow Apollos"; another, "I follow Cephas"; still another, "I follow Christ." Is Christ divided? (1 Corinthians 1:11–13a).*

The Church, which is the body of Christ, must practice *cohesion*. Jesus said that our love for one another would be the mark of a true disciple. The world will judge whether or not we are His disciples by the love we demonstrate for one another (John 13:34–35). Factions and schisms harm the testimony of Christ. This is especially true at a military base or post or on a ship, all relatively small communities. Christians must make every effort to coordinate their efforts and cooperate with other believers in their community. Nothing harms the name of Christ as much as His disciples leveling their "guns" at each other. If Christ is our supreme Commander and we are all in His army, we need to coordinate our actions with our allies. This principle applies not only to individuals but also to chapels, churches, and Christian organizations. Regardless of denomination or affiliation, Christians must visibly demonstrate their unity and cooperation to the watching world.

**Security** (Defensive)—To maintain offensive military action, fighting forces must be defended from enemy attack. This involves gaining information about the enemy and ensuring that weak points are adequately defended. *Security* aims to protect forces from surprise action and to minimize losses. It is maintained only by constant vigilance on the part of every warrior.

> *Be self-controlled and alert. Your enemy the devil prowls around like a roaring lion looking for someone to devour (1 Peter 5:8).*

Even though we have a very real and potent spiritual enemy, "we are not unaware of his schemes" (2 Corinthians 2:11). Christians have the potential to win every engagement with their enemy. Victory depends on using the full armor of God (Ephesians 6) and being empowered by God's Holy Spirit. Why, then, do so many Christians fall? They ignore the principle of *security*. They plan their own *initiatives* but fail to account for and protect against the attacks of the enemy. Christians who are cut off from fellowship or who are out of communication with their Commander are especially vulnerable to attack.

*So, if you think you are standing firm, be careful that you don't fall! (1 Corinthians 10:12).*

*Therefore, my brothers, be all the more eager to make your calling and election sure. For if you do these things, you will never fall (2 Peter 1:10).*

**Simplicity**—This principle requires all commands, strategies, plans, tactics, and procedures to be clear, simple, and unencumbered. *Simplicity* promotes understanding, reduces confusion, and permits easy execution. *Simplicity* seeks to reduce to a minimum words, equipment, procedures, and steps in order to reduce the total number of "moving parts" in the complex machinery of warfare.

*"Martha, Martha," the Lord answered, "you are worried and upset about many things, but only one thing is needed. Mary has chosen what is better, and it will not be taken away from her" (Luke 10:41–42).*

Our lives easily become cluttered with activities and possessions, leaving us rich in things and poor in spirit and character. Christians need to periodically assess their level of clutter and distraction and make adjustments. In the intense lifestyle of a warrior, clutter cannot be tolerated. Imagine the Sergeant Major telling everyone to gather their equipment for a 3-day, 70-mile march. Knowing you had to carry everything you brought, you would choose your items selectively, bringing only the bare necessities.

Your life can get weighed down with activities, possessions, and debt. You can fill your free time with commitments to things of little eternal value. To live a victorious life in an already complex occupation, simplify your life and lighten your load. Be sure to know a simple, easy-to-understand presentation of the Gospel message. The Gospel is simple and powerful; don't rob it of its power by making it complex and dull. Have a few clear goals for your physical and spiritual progress. Be very good at a few things rather than dabbling in many. Like Mary, consciously choose to do what is better.

**Surprise**—*Surprise* means to initiate action at a time, place, or in a manner that the enemy is neither prepared for nor expects. It is achieved through audacity, originality, innovation, and timely execution. *Surprise* can decisively shift the balance of power, giving the attacking forces the advantage of seizing the *initiative* while forcing the enemy to react. *Surprise* does not guarantee victory, but it does give great advantage.

*And they were* completely flabbergasted, *and that in a super-abundant degree which itself was augmented by the addition of yet more* astonishment, *saying, He [Jesus] has done all things well! (Mark 7:37a, WUEST, emphasis added).*

*When they saw the courage of Peter and John and real-ized that they were unschooled, ordinary men, they were* astonished *and they took note that these men had been with Jesus (Acts 4:13, emphasis added).*

Jesus' life and teaching were astonishing. He was not what people expected in a Messiah. He surprised people. The woman at the well was surprised that Jesus spoke to her. The woman caught in adultery was surprised that Jesus did not condemn her. Satan and his host were surprised when Jesus rose from the dead.

A true Christian will always be a *surprise* to the watching world, just as Peter and John astonished their peers. The world believes Christians are simple, sad, and rigid. When we live authentic, obedient lives, as Jesus did, we catch people by *surprise*.

Satan tells the world lies about Jesus and His followers. As you live your life before the watching world, the reality of a true Christian's life will amaze and attract others. *Surprise* is a powerful force in Christian warfare. Don't be afraid to use it.

**Concentration** (Mass)—Overwhelming numbers at every point along a battlefront are not necessary. The principle of *concentration* teaches the commander to gather superior forces at places of highest priority. Mass coupled with *initiative* allows the attacking force to concentrate at points of advantage and forces the enemy to disperse his force to cover known and possible points of combat. Mass does not always require numerical advantage. Forces effectively massed and supported can defeat larger numbers, particularly if the attacking force uses *surprise* as well.

*"Again, I tell you that if two of you on earth agree about anything you ask for, it will be done for you by my Father in heaven. For where two or three come together in my name, there am I with them" (Matthew 18:19–20).*

It has been said, "God and one committed follower constitute a majority!" It does not take hundreds of Christians massed together to impact a military unit. One or two who are committed to the Lord and to one another can accomplish a lot. You don't need to wait for huge groups of believers to form before you attempt to live as a Christian witness to others. God's promise is for "two or three."

Of course, there is also benefit from periodically massing believers at a base, post, or ship. One large base gathered congregations from several worship services in the gym once a quarter for a mass worship and praise service. Seeing so many Christians together stirs the heart and fuels the soul for action. There are times to be encouraged by a crowd of believers and times when only two or three are needed to accomplish God's purpose.

**Economy of Force**—To mass force at one point, other places must be manned with a minimum number of combatants. The greatest possible force is committed to the highest priority *objective*. The wise commander understands that there is never enough manpower or equipment to simultaneously achieve every *objective*. Commanders are forced to choose from among many worthy *objectives*. Failure to economize will dilute the strength of the army and lead to defeat.

*"Martha, Martha," the Lord answered, "you are worried and upset about many things, but only* one thing is needed" *(Luke 10:41–42a, emphasis added).*

Maybe you've heard the expression, "Only one life, will soon be past; only what's done for Christ will last." All Christians eventually realize they have limited capacity. Some, however, burn out before they realize it. This is why *economy of force* is so important. It's easy to get involved in many good activities but to have little impact. The *good* is always the enemy of the *best*. Instead, focus on your highest priorities and ensure that the best of your time is allotted to these. Understand your gifting and capacities. Develop the habit of saying "no" to opportunities that use your time and resources with little substantial return on your investment.

Every choice to do one thing is also a choice not to do other things. Your time, money, emotions, creativity, and physical energy are all limited. Concentrate your best resources on God's highest priorities.

**Pursuit** (Exploitation)—This principle encourages follow-up of each breakthrough. The commander who achieves a victory will continue to press the enemy and exploit the gains he has made. Failure to pursue the fight to the end can result in fighting the same foe again, perhaps on less favorable terms the next time. *Pursuit* means finishing what was begun as quickly as possible.

> *Not that I have already obtained all this, or have already been made perfect, but I press on to take hold of that for which Christ Jesus took hold of me. Brothers, I do not consider myself yet to have taken hold of it. But one thing I do: Forgetting what is behind and straining toward what is ahead, I press on toward the goal to win the prize for which God has called me heavenward in Christ Jesus (Philippians 3:12–14).*

*Pursuit* has several applications in spiritual warfare. First, it means we follow-up and disciple new believers. We wouldn't fight to win a battle and then fail to pursue it to the end. Yet we often do precisely that with new Christians. We pray for their conversion, share the Gospel, even lead them to Christ, but fail to maximize this victory with follow-up.

*Pursuit* in spiritual warfare also applies to continuing on, day by day, in victory. We are never to let down our guard. We never "retire" and rest on our laurels. From the day we enter His service to the day we enter eternity, we pursue His purpose with our whole lives. Keep on keeping on.

> *Let us not become weary in doing good, for at the proper time we will reap a harvest if we do not give up (Galatians 6:9).*

## STAYING TRUE TO THE PRINCIPLES

The Principles of War offer time-proven wisdom. Those who ignore the accumulated experience of previous warriors will generally finish poorly. Success and victory will generally favor those who study and apply these time-tested principles.

Perhaps the best-known treatise on the Principles of War is by Karl von Clausewitz. In his 1832 book, originally titled *The Most Important Principles for the Conduct of War to Complete My Course of Instruction of His Royal Highness the Crown Prince*, he conveyed to the Prussian Crown Prince Frederick William all the lessons he had learned about warfare. He taught most of the principles discussed in this chapter. At the end of the book, he made this important observation:

> "These principles are within the reach of any well-organized mind, which is unprejudiced and not entirely unfamiliar with the subject. Even the application of these principles on maps or on paper presents no difficulty, and to have devised a good plan of operation is no great masterpiece. The great difficulty is this: *To remain faithful throughout to the principles we have laid down for ourselves!*" (emphasis added).

The apostle Paul reminded his readers of the same thing. He said it this way:

> *Therefore, my dear brothers, stand firm. Let nothing move you. Always give yourselves fully to the work of the Lord, because you know that your labor in the Lord is not in vain (1 Corinthians 15:58).*

Knowing and understanding these basic principles of victorious Christian living is the first step. Commit yourself each day to consistent obedience, applying what you know and teaching others by your speech and your example.

 **SUMMARY**

⊕ The Principles of War are time-proven foundations established for conducting successful warfare.

⊕ As a Christian soldier, you will benefit from knowing and applying these principles to the spiritual warfare you face in your own life.

⊕ Victory in this war is assured if you align your efforts with your Commander, Jesus Christ.

# Onward Christian Soldiers

*Onward Christian soldiers*
*Marching as to war*
*With the cross of Jesus*
*Going on before.*

IN THIS FAMILIAR SONG, WE USUALLY think of "Christian soldiers" as men and women from all walks of life who serve in the army of God. In this book, however, we're talking about Christian soldiers literally—men and women who follow Christ and also serve in their country's military forces. As a Christian soldier, you follow two banners, the banner of Jesus' cross and the banner of your nation. Following Jesus and serving honorably in the military are compatible pursuits. The high military standards of integrity, service, responsibility, and sacrifice parallel the standards Jesus established for His disciples.

Christians in the military serve both the nation that enlisted or commissioned them and the Lord Jesus who saved them and called them into His service. As you follow the banner of your branch of service, you are reminded of the traditions and honorable deeds that warriors like you have accomplished over the past 200 years. When you look to the Christian banner, your perspective changes. The banner of Christ has been flying for more than 2,000 years. Before the United States was a nation, God was enlisting and commissioning soldiers in His army. Over the millennia, thousands have paid the ultimate price for serving God. Their legacy of righteousness and service challenges all who follow to reach for higher levels of character and action.

> *Therefore, since we are surrounded by such a great cloud of witnesses, let us throw off everything that hinders and the sin that so easily entangles, and let us run with perseverance the race marked out for us. Let us fix our eyes on Jesus, the author and perfecter of our faith, who for the joy set before him endured the cross, scorning its shame, and sat down at the right hand of the throne of God. Consider him who endured such opposition from sinful men, so that you will not grow weary and lose heart (Hebrews 12:1–3).*

## KEYS TO SUCCESS

God desires that we serve Him, as well as our earthly superiors, honorably and that we finish our earthly tasks well. Those who are successful at this share three core characteristics: balance, wisdom, and endurance.

### *Balance*

Balance is the ability to see the extremes at either end and find the appropriate middle ground. Every issue of life can be taken to extremes, either too much or too little. The book of Proverbs is filled with warnings against extremes. The author of the following proverb asks God for balance.

> *"Give me neither poverty nor riches, but give me only my daily bread. Otherwise, I may have too much and disown you and say, 'Who is the LORD?' Or I may become poor and steal, and so dishonor the name of my God"* *(Proverbs 30:8–9).*

We can pursue too much or too little of everything God gives us to enjoy. We can have too much or too little money, affection, work, recreation, fellowship, speech, or pride. But men and women who spend their lives in fellowship with God increasingly find balance in every facet of life.

An orbiting satellite demonstrates perfect balance. The rate at which it speeds forward and the rate at which it falls toward the earth are equal; therefore, it stays in orbit. An orbiting object that loses balance either flies off into space or burns up as it plunges to the earth. Christians who maintain a close relationship with God are able to avoid the extremes that lead to destruction. A balanced life brings stability and provides a powerful testimony for those who live at the extremes.

### *Wisdom*

Wisdom is the ability to see the circumstances, comprehend the issues, and consistently make the right decisions. Wisdom is an art, developed over time by those who pursue it. God offers to train us in His wisdom when we read His Word, observe life's experiences, and follow the prompting of His Spirit. Consider this invitation to wisdom:

> *Wisdom has built her house; she has hewn out its seven pillars. . . . "Let all who are simple come in here!" she says to those who lack judgment. . . . "Leave your simple ways and you will live; walk in the way of understanding. . . . The fear of the LORD is the beginning of wisdom, and knowledge of the Holy One is understanding" (Proverbs 9:1, 4, 6, 10).*

The military is an extremely demanding profession. It requires rigorous training and unquestioning discipline. Physical, moral, and ethical choices abound. By the power and leading of God, a soldier can plot a course through the canyons of decision and end well. God will train those who seek wisdom.

Wisdom exercised by the godly warrior benefits everyone involved and adds to the whole organization. The book of Galatians instructs us this way:

> *Since we live by the Spirit, let us keep in step with the Spirit (Galatians 5:25).*

This is a military command: Keep in step! Wisdom, at its core, is keeping in step with the will of God and the prompting of His Spirit.

### Endurance

Endurance means sticking to the important goals and commitments in life. The military encourages endurance. In almost every competitive endeavor, including combat, victory smiles on the tenacious. The ability to endure more than was thought possible lies within each of us, but it must be stirred up. The Bible talks about endurance this way:

> *Let us not become weary in doing good, for at the proper time we will reap a harvest if we do not give up (Galatians 6:9).*

> *Therefore, my dear brothers, stand firm. Let nothing move you. Always give yourselves fully to the work of the Lord, because you know that your labor in the Lord is not in vain (1 Corinthians 15:58).*

Christians are encouraged to keep doing the right thing until their last day. The Christian warrior is equally admonished to remain faithful in service to both the banner of the nation and the cross of Christ. Among the great heroes of the faith are three similar men: Joseph, Nehemiah, and Daniel. All three served faithfully in a foreign culture, maintaining a reputation for job effectiveness and personal integrity. They endured in the face of overwhelming opposition. Follow in their footsteps. Make these qualities your own.

If God has called you to service in the military, you are traveling on a path of rich opportunity and exciting challenges. Carefully prepare for each step—from basic training to specialty schools, from professional leadership schools to combat simulators. Prepare also for the awesome responsibility of representing the life of Jesus to people who are looking for "ultimate" answers. As you follow closely in the Master's will and Word, God will use you wonderfully, in His service.

*There's a Royal Banner given for display*
*To the soldiers of the King*
*As an ensign fair we lift it up today*
*While as ransomed ones we sing.*
*Marching on, marching on*
*For Christ count everything but loss;*
*But to crown Him King*
*Toil and sing*
*'Neath the Banner of the Cross.*

# Also Available From Dawson Media

### Discovery: God's Answers to Our Deepest Questions

This intensive Bible study addresses a Christian's basic questions about God and the kind of abiding relationship He wants with us. Covers such topics as, "Is God really in control?" "Does He have a purpose for my life?" and "How do I know if my faith is growing?" For new and seasoned believers, *Discovery* is ideal for small groups or individual use. 235 pages

*By Will Wyatt*

### One-Verse Evangelism

*One-Verse Evangelism* is a simple, interactive way to share Christ's love conversationally and visually using just one verse, Romans 6:23. Thousands have used it to introduce their friends to the Gospel of Christ. 18 pages

*By Randy Raysbrook*

### Now That I Am Born Again

This pocket-size booklet, designed as a monthly devotional, will walk you through the book of Ephesians, building your confidence in your new identity in Christ. Ideal for small groups, Sunday school classes, or as a gift to encourage other believers. 36 pages

*By David Lyons*

### The Five Legacies of The Navigators

This booklet offers a look at the spiritual heritage of The Navigators. Lorne Sanny teaches on five key elements of following Christ with passion and dedication. 12 pages

*By Lorne Sanny*

### Meditation

This Navigator classic has helped thousands enter into a more abiding relationship with Christ through meditation on the Word. 96 pages

*By Jim Downing*

### 23 Ways to Jump-Start Your Spiritual Battery

Feeling stalled in your walk with the Lord? Randy Raysbrook offers 23 creative ways to revive your zest for Christ. 8 pages, 5/pack

*By Randy Raysbrook*

### The Nuts and Bolts of One-to-One Discipling

Packed with the discipleship basics Navigators have used for decades, *Nuts and Bolts* provides what you need to effectively disciple another believer. 20 pages, 5/pack

*By Tom Yeakley*

## To order additional copies of *In His Service,* or for more information on any of our products, or to request a catalog:

**Go online:** www.dawsonmedia.com

**Write to:** Dawson Media · P.O. Box 6000 · Colorado Springs, CO 80934

**Call toll-free:** (888) 547-9635

**Fax:** (719) 594-2553

## dawsonmedia

*Dawson Media aims to help Navigator staff and laypeople create and experiment with new ministry tools for personal evangelism and discipleship.*